DERBYSHI
— an A to

by
JOHN N. MERRILL

Maps and Photographs by John N. Merrill

a J.N.M. PUBLICATION

1989

a J.N.M. PUBLICATION

JNM PUBLICATIONS,
WINSTER,
MATLOCK,
DERBYSHIRE.
DE4 2DQ

This book is copyright under the Berne Convention. All rights are reserved. Apart from any fair dealing for the purposes of private study, research, criticism or review, as permitted under the Copyright Act, 1956, no part of this publication may be reproduced, stored in a retrieval system, or transmitted in any other form by any means, electronic, electrical, chemical, mechanical, optical, photocopying, recording or otherwise, without the prior permission of the copyright owner. Enquiries should be addressed to the publishers.

Conceived, edited, typeset, designed, marketed and distributed by John N. Merrill.

©Text — John N. Merrill 1989

©Maps and photographs — John N. Merrill 1989

First Published — October 1983 — ISBN 0 907496 11 3

This enlarged edition — February 1989

ISBN 0 907496 71 7

Meticulous research has been undertaken to ensure that this publication is highly accurate at the time of going to press. The publishers, however, cannot be held responsible for alterations, errors or omissions, but they would welcome notification of such for future editions.

Printed by: Amadeus Press, Huddersfield. W. Yorks.

Set in Rockwell: Light, Medium and Bold.

Cover sketches by John Creber. Front cover — Peacock Inn, Oakerthorpe. Back cover — Winster Hall Inn sign.

ABOUT JOHN N. MERRILL

John combines the characteristics and strength of a mountain climber with the stamina and athletic capabilities of a marathon runner. In this respect he is unique and has to his credit a whole string of remarkable long walks. He is without question the world's leading marathon walker.

Over the last fifteen years he has walked more than 100,000 miles and successfully completed ten walks of at least 1,000 miles or more.

His six major walks in Great Britain are —
- Hebridean Journey .... 1,003 miles
- Northern Isles Journey .... 913 miles
- Irish Island Journey .... 1,578 miles
- Parkland Journey .... 2,043 miles
- Lands End to John o'Groats .... 1,608 miles

and in 1978 he became the first person (permanent Guinness Book of Records entry) to walk the entire coastline of Britain — 6,824 miles in ten months.

In Europe he has walked across Austria — 712 miles — hiked the Tour of Mont Blanc, completed High Level Routes in the Dolomites and Italian Alps, and the GR20 route across Corsica in training! In 1982 he walked across Europe — 2,806 miles in 107 days — crossing seven countries, the Swiss and French Alps and the complete Pyrennean chain — the hardest and longest mountain walk in Europe, with more than 600,000 feet of ascent!

In America he used the the world's longest footpath — The Appalachian Trail — 2,200 miles — as a training walk. He has walked from Mexico to Canada via the Pacific Crest Trail in record time — 118 days for 2,700 miles. In Canada he has walked the Rideau Trail.

During the summer of 1984, John set off from Virginia Beach on the Atlantic coast, and walked 4,226 miles without a rest day, across the width of America to Santa Cruz and San Francisco on the Pacific Ocean. His walk is unquestionably his greatest achievement, being, in modern history, the longest, hardest crossing of the USA in the shortest time — under six months (178 days). The direct distance is 2,800 miles.

Between major walks John is out training in his own area — the Peak District National Park. As well as walking in other parts of Britain and Europe he has been trekking in the Himalayas five times. He has created more than ten challenge walks which have been used to raise more than 250,000 for charity. From his own walks he raised over 80,000. He is author of more than ninety books, most of which he publishes himself. His book sales are in excess of 2 million.

CONTENTS

	Page No
INTRODUCTION	1
ORIGIN OF INN SIGNS	2
NOTES ON BREWING	4
A TO Z GUIDE TO INNS	8
LOST INNS	63
INNS VISIT RECORD CHART	66
OTHER BOOKS BY JOHN MERRILL	74

QUOTE :–

The Green Man — Ashbourne

Ashbourne, September 26th, 1777.

After breakfast I departed and pursued my journey northwards. I took my postchaise from The Green Man, a very good inn at Ashbourne, the mistress of which, a mighty civil gentlewoman, curtseying very low, presented me with an engraving of the sign of her house; to which she had subjoined, in her own handwriting, an address in such singular simplicity of style, that I have preserved it pasted upon one of the boards of my original journal.

James Boswell

▲ GLOSSOP
▲ ASHOPTON WOODLANDS
▲ HAYFIELD
▲ NEW MILLS ▲ EDALE
CASTLETON ▲ ▲ HOPE ▲ BAMFORD
BRADWELL ▲ ▲ HATHERSAGE
▲ WHALEY BRIDGE LONGSHAW ▲ ▲ DRONFIELD
▲ CHAPEL EN LE FRITH
▲ FROGGATT EDGE
▲ TAXAL ▲ STONEY MIDDLETON
▲ BUXTON ▲ TIDESWELL
HASSOP ▲ ▲ BASLOW ▲ BOLSOVER
EARL STERNDALE ▲ ▲ BAKEWELL ▲ CHESTERFIELD
▲ MONYASH ▲ HOLYMOORSIDE
▲ CROWDICOTE ▲ BARLBOROUGH
▲ NORTH WINGFIELD
▲ YOULGREAVE ▲ CLAY CROSS
HARTINGTON ▲ ▲ WINSTER
BONSALL ▲ ▲ MATLOCK BATH
OAKERTHORPE ▲ ▲ ALFRETON
BRASSINGTON ▲ ▲ WIRKSWORTH

▲ THORPE
▲ BELPER ▲ LANGLEY MILL
ASHBOURNE ▲
▲ WINDLEY
▲ DUFFIELD ▲ ILKESTON
▲ BRAILSFORD
QUARNDON ▲ ▲ SPONDON
▲ DERBY

N

▲ SUDBURY ▲ ETWALL ▲ SHARDLOW
▲ WILLINGTON
REPTON ▲ ▲ MELBOURNE
▲ TICKNALL
▲ SWADLINCOTE

▲ INNS SITUATED AT

INTRODUCTION

One's first thought at writing a book such as this is, what a marvellous excuse to go on a very extended pub crawl, but in reality it has proved a lengthy task. Exploring the county on foot, photographing and researching each inn's history. I have doubled the content from the first edition which has necessitated two years of very enjoyable research. The scope is tremendous and in the end I have had to shut my eyes to others to learn about. My interest lies in the history of the building. This I feel is a fascinating study, especially in a county already so rich in historical buildings.

To have carried out a complete survey of the entire county would have been a mammoth task, and I could not have done justice to it in the space allowed. My plan of action therefore was to include all the most interesting inns, in relation to history, legend, oddities and unique attributes. It is purely a random selection, and my apologies for missing your favourite one.

The history of the buildings is a rewarding subject. Some have been old coaching inns, others have been churches before becoming an inn, several are named after a particular event, while others are named after the Lord of the Manor. Many are situated in wild remote places, while others are on a busy road and often overlooked. I hope the book gives you a new slant into the exploration of this exceptional county. If the inn stocks your favourite fluid and serves a tasty meal, then the visit has been even more worthwhile. Happy exploring!

John N. Merrill

John N. Merrill
Winster.

Derbyshire has five licensing districts, which are as follows:-

	Division served	No. of full On-Licences
1.	Alfreton, Belper and Matlock. (Alfreton & Belper 141 & Matlock 202)	343
2.	Ashbourne, Derby County, Appletree and South Derbyshire	275
3.	Chesterfield and Bakewell	416
4.	Glossop and High Peak (Glossop 54, High Peak 126)	180
5.	Ilkeston	214
		1,428

Origin of Inn Signs

The origins date back to the 13th Century when it became law that a pole should be placed jutting out from the building to indicate that a new brew had been made. The authorities would then call to check it. At first it was only the main taverns and inns that had poles. Smaller places where they brewed their own, had a bush or a broom of twigs placed over the door, known as ale stakes. As the alehouses grew in numbers, signs were added for identification to the poles, such as stars. These eventually became more elaborate, such as the Green Man inn sign in Ashbourne. In turn they progressed to today's hanging square sign.

Before the Black Death, 1348-50, the price for a gallon of ordinary ale was 1/2d. In 1577, Sir Francis Leake of Sutton Scarsdale was asked to take a census of the ale houses in Derbyshire. He found that Chesterfield with a population of 4,000 had 68 and one large inn. Derby too had 68 and seven large inns.

INN NAMES —

The Peacock is the most common name in Derbyshire with about fifty inns so called. The Bull's Head and New Inn number over thirty a piece. With more than twenty each are The Red Lion, The Crown, The Railway Inn, The White Hart, The Nag's Head, and The Duke of Devonshire. There are more than a dozen Blue Bell Inn's and only three Robin Hood Inns. The most popular name in Britain is, The Red Lion, with approximately 650!

A few notes on what their name means or is derived from:-

ALBERT INN — A mark of respect to the Prince Consort, husband of Queen Victoria.

THE ANCHOR — A place of rest and security for travellers.

THE ANGEL — meant to represent the angel saluting the blessed Virgin.

BARLEY MOW — meaning a rick of barley from which ale used to be brewed. Mow is pronounced to rhyme with cow.

THE BULL — refers to bull baiting, which ceased in the early 19th Century. Several bull rings still exist in Derbyshire, such as at Eyam, Snitterton and Foolow.

THE CASTLE — after Eleanor of Castile, the wife of Edward I. Their arms included a three-towered castle.

THE COCK AND THE FIGHTING COCK — named after the once popular sport and pastime, cock fighting.

CROSS KEYS — refers to the two iron and golden keys of St. Peter. A common sign before the Reformation.

THE CROWN — very ancient sign in honour of the sovereign. One London landlord of a Crown Inn said his son was heir to the crown. He was committed to prison for the insult during the reign of Edward IV — 1461–1483.

DOG AND DUCK — refers to a rather brutal 18th Century sport when a tethered duck was chased over a pond by dogs.

THE GRAPES — possibly refers to a famous drink called Derby Sack, a dry wine of Elizabethan days.

OLD FEATHERS — derived from the badge of Arthur Tudor, elder brother of Henry VIII.

THE PEACOCK — badge of the Manner's family (Haddon Hall)

SARACENS HEAD AND TURK'S HEAD — named as a result of the Crusades.

THE SUN — from the rising sun, a former Yorkist badge.

THE THREE TUNS — the arms of the Vintners Company.

THE VOLUNTEER — named after the volunteer movement of Victoria's reign.

PEACOCK HOTEL, OAKERTHORPE

A few notes on Malthouses and Brewing in Derbyshire

> "Of this strange Drink, so like the Stygian Lake,
> Men call it ale, I know not what to make;
> They drink it thick, and piss it wondrous thin;
> What store of Dregs must needs remain within?"
>
> > Henry of Auranches, Poet Laureat
> > to Henry III, referring to Derby
> > ale.

Derby ale was widely known in the 18th Century. Fuller says, Never was the wine of Falernam better known to the Romans than the canary of Derby to the English. John Houghton F.R.S., in his weekly Collection for the Improvement of Husbandry and Trade, recorded in 1693 that there were seventy six malthouses in Derby. Each week these malthouses made enough for the town plus 300 loads (each equal to six bushels, 49 gallons) which were transported to Cheshire and Lancashire.

Glover stated that in the early seventeenth century The chief trade (of Derby) consisted in malting and brewing ale which was in great request and much celebrated in London to which city large quantities were sent. Such fame inevitably brought the town a bad name, as Hutton mentioned in his History of Derby published in 1791 — All the writers mention Derby as famous for Ale; consequently for drunkards; for the lower class ever want a little more than they can get. The latter half of last century saw Derby as a major producer of ale. Today the once-famous brewing city is dry, for there is no brewery here, and nearby Burton-upon-Trent, just inside Staffordshire, has become the centre. One reason for this is because the Abbots of Burton-upon-Trent discovered they had the best water for brewing ale in the world. One or two Derby inns may still make their own brew, but that is all that is left of a once large and prosperous industry.

In Derby can be seen a malthouse in Manchester Street which now serves as a chemical manufactory. Another is the Meeting House in St. Michael's Lane. There are others outside the city, at such places as Little Eaton, Shardlow and Bull Bridge. Derby is believed to have been the first place to use coke in the malt drying process, in about 1643. John Houghton observed in 1963 that: The reason for Derby malt being so fine and sweet is the drying of it with cowks, which is a sort of cole. The method of brewing in the late 17th Century was again recorded by Houghton:-

> "The malt thus prepared is mashed with boyling liquor so
> as it may easily be stir'd about with the mashrule and
> having stood close covered about 2 hours (in which time
> more boyling liquor is got ready) it must be run off, and
> so much more hot liquor put on as will serve to fill the
> Vessel or Wessels designed: which a tryal or two by the
> Brewing Vessels will easily discover.
> To a Hogshead of the first running is put about one pound
> of Hops; when as much Wort is gathered as will serve for
> the Ale, then the grains must be filled up again with
> boyling liquor and so stand about half an hour and then
> let run off which will make good Beer, the Grains filled

up again and standing so another half hour or more, will make small Beer very well worth boyling.
The Ale or best Wort must boyl an Hour and half to two Hours before it be laded into the Cooler, and when it is cold enough, Yeast must be put to it. If it be good Wort and well boyled, it will have an Oyl upon it, which you may perceive by rubbing it between your Forefinger and Thumb."

Except for a few instances, the method of brewing remained the same and was carried on in as many as twenty inns in Derby, twenty five years ago. The Crystal Palace, Derby, had been brewing its own ale since it opened in 1869. In 1961 the owner was brewing 200 gallons at a time. The Seven Stars in King Street, Derby, had been brewing for nearly 300 years, from 1680 to 1962. The Friary, one of the last survivors of the local art, was selling its own ale, known as 'Hadfield's Home Brew' after the owner, and sold for 8d. (3p.) less per pint in 1962 than the mass-produced brands. The Exeter Arms in Exeter Street was brewing until 1969; the landlady, Miss Winifred Jackson, was the only woman in Derby to hold a brewer's licence.

On a much larger scale there were several breweries in Derby producing a wide range of ales. One of the largest and oldest was Alton and Co. Ltd., the Wardwick Brewery, which was founded in 1788 by Thomas Lowe. Upon his death his son took over in 1828, and when he died the business was purchased by William Alton and Edward Barrett in 1869. William Alton later became the sole owner, and the brewery became a limited company in 1887. The factory was enlarged, and became one of the most efficient in the country. Water for the ale came from wells within the premises or from tanks connected to the Derby Waterworks. The malt cleaning and crushing rooms were on the top floor. As you moved downwards the various stages of production were passed, with the cellars in the basement. The final drying of the malt was carefully controlled, as this produced the various colours of the ales.

THE DERBY BREWERY COMPANY,

Other Derby breweries included the Derby Brewery Company on Nottingham Road. This concern was started in the 1830s by Robert Clarke, and the name was changed in 1890. 'Derby Ales' was one of the main products. On the Ashbourne road was Stretton's Derby Brewery Ltd., established in about 1860. As well as making their own ales and stouts, they bottled both Bass and Guinness. In 1877 Offiler's Brewery was started at Vine End, Whittaker Street. Seven years later, in 1884, the business moved to Ambrose Street, where they remained until the brewery closed and merged with Charrington's in 1965. One reason for closing was that the equipment had ended its serviceable life and the cost of replacement would have been prohibitive.

Beer was also made near Chapel-en-le-Frith at Brook House Farm, near Combs, and was sold locally. An artificial lake in the garden of the Old Brook House supplied the pure water to the brewery, until it ceased operating in 1857. Brampton, near Chesterfield, also had a brewery about this time. The pipe factory there was purchased in 1878 by Charles Hames Chater, Harold Soames and Frederick William Soames for 594. They were described as 'Common Brewers' and traded under the name of 'Brampton Brewery Company'. And at the beginning of this century there were two other breweries in the Chesterfield area — J.J. Clayton, Mineral Water manufacturers, brewers of the celebrated stone ginger beer and hop bitters, and ale and stout bottlers, of Standard Works, Whittington Moor, Chesterfield; whilst operating from 113 Salter Gate were Messrs. Simmonite and Sons, Mineral Water manufacturers and hop bitter brewers.

EXCAVATOR INN, WINGFIELD PARK (NR AMBERGATE)

GREEN MAN AND BLACK HEAD, ASHBOURNE

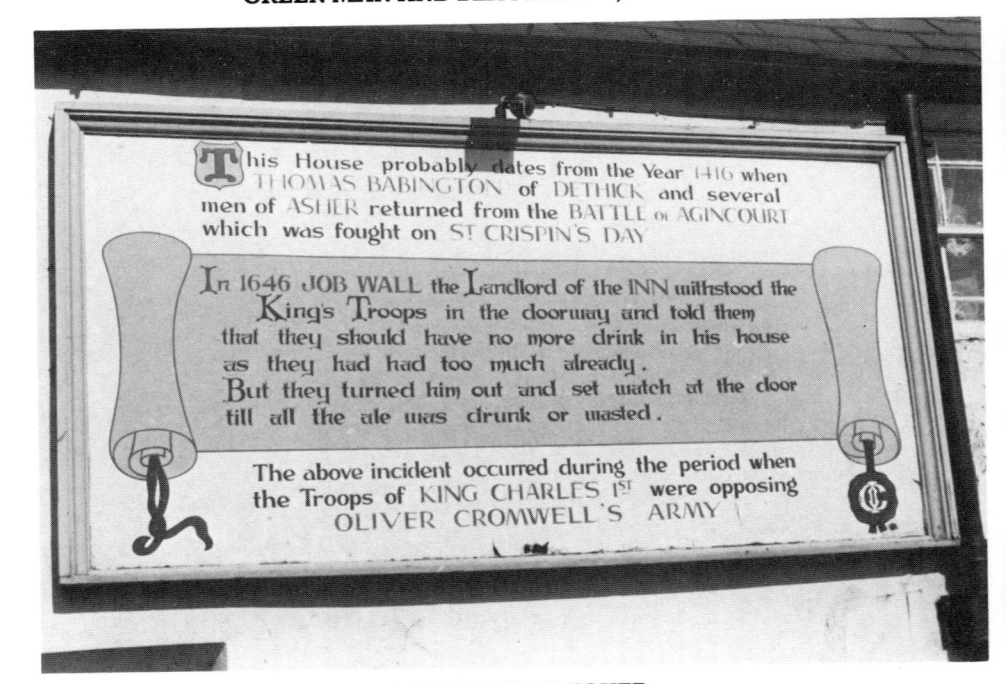

This House probably dates from the Year 1416 when THOMAS BABINGTON of DETHICK and several men of ASHER returned from the BATTLE of AGINCOURT which was fought on St CRISPIN'S DAY

In 1646 JOB WALL the Landlord of the INN withstood the King's Troops in the doorway and told them that they should have no more drink in his house as they had had too much already. But they turned him out and set watch at the door till all the ale was drunk or wasted.

The above incident occurred during the period when the Troops of KING CHARLES 1st were opposing OLIVER CROMWELL'S ARMY

CRISPIN INN, ASHOVER

A

ALDERWASLEY

YE OLDE BEAR INN, ALDERWASLEY. G.R. 31452 — A 16th century coaching inn and Post House lying on the Birmingham-Derby-Chesterfield-Sheffield turnpike. In the mid-18th Century a stage coach service ran along this route. The overnight stop was in Derby, breakfast in Matlock, dinner in Chesterfield, and reaching Sheffield later that night.

ALFRETON

THE ANGEL HOTEL, KING STREET, ALFRETON — Sir Francis Leake's survey of alehouses, inns and taverns in the Scarsdale Hundred in 1577 showed that Alfreton had one inn — The Angel — and that the innkeeper was William Teilier. The present Angel Hotel occupies the same site. The original Angel was the former townhouse of the Abbot of Beauchief (Sheffield) and was sold at the dissolution of the Abbey. For the survey an inn was described as a public house for the lodging and entertainment of travellers. An alehouse was a place which had a J.P.'s licence to sell ale.

AMBERGATE

EXCAVATOR INN, BUCKLAND HOLLOW, AMBERGATE — One of the most unusual pubs in Derbyshire, with a JCB on top; hence the name.

HURT ARMS HOTEL, AMBERGATE — Stands on the site of a thatched inn and built in 1876.

ASHBOURNE

THE GREEN MAN INN, ST. JOHN STREET, ASHBOURNE — A mid-18th Century coaching inn with a coach entrance to a covered court. James Boswell was here in 1777 and described it as a very good Inn, where the landlady, a mighty civil gentlewoman, curtseying very low, presented me with an engraving of the sign of her house. The inn sign is very unusual, and is one of only six signs left in the country. The gallows sign bridges the street and really commemmorates the amalgamation of two inns — the Green Man and the Black's Head — in 1825. The site of the Black's Head has now been converted into shops, but the inn had one of three cockpits that existed in the town in the 18th Century. The inn sign has the words — The Green Man and Black's Head. The word royal was added after Princess Victoria stopped briefly while passing through Ashbourne in the 1830s. This sign illustrates a green man on one side and a hunting scene on the other. Above the centre of the cross piece is a two faced blackamoor' head. On one side he is smiling and on the other frowning.

The Green Man, which is a popular inn sign, is Jack-in-the-Green. In Ashbourne Church one of the pillar capitals of the nave has a 'green man' carved upon it. The Green Man is often referred to as the May King. In the church he is covered with hawthorn leaves and only his face is exposed.

PLOUGH INN, OLD DERBY ROAD, ASHBOURNE — Ashbourne is famed for its Shrovetide football match between the uppards and downards; depending on what side of Henmore Brook you were born on. This pub is the headquarters of the downards, with a large collection of Shrovetide trophies including four footballs given by the people who scored with them.

SMITH'S TAVERN, ST. JOHN'S STREET, ASHBOURNE — The oldest pub in Ashbourne. In 1963 a runaway lorry badly damaged the front.

WELLINGTON INN, ST. JOHN STREET, ASHBOURNE — formerly known as the Nag's Head but renamed after the Battle of Waterloo on June 18th 1815.

ASHOPTON WOODLANDS

SNAKE INN, ASHOPTON WOODLANDS. G.R. 113905 — Situated 1,086 feet above sea level on the Snake Road (A57), this inn can safely be referred to as the remotest and loneliest in the county. In the early 19th Century the volume of trade between Sheffield and Manchester was growing rapidly. The traffic route was via Castleton. A more direct route was needed, and in 1818 Parliament gave its blessing to a route over the Snake Pass. Thomas Telford was the engineer, and the road reaches a height of 1,680 feet and was, at the time, one of the highest turnpike roads in England. Just before the road was opened in 1821, an inn was built at the head of Woodlands Valley through which the road runs. At first the inn was named Lady Clough House after the nearby clough, but as a mark of respect to the Duke of Devonshire it was renamed the Snake Inn. Part of the Devonshire crest is a snake. The first landlord was John Longden, a Methodist preacher, who held prayer meetings here. The field in front of the inn was where prize fights were held.

ASHOVER

THE CRISPIN INN, ASHOVER — Much of the history of the inn is detailed on the large board on the front of the building. It is generally accepted that the inn dates from 1416 when Thomas Babington and others returned home after the Battle of Agincourt, fought on St. Crispin's Day (25th October). The nearby church, dedicated to All Saints, has amongst its treasures a splendid alabaster tomb to another Thomas Babington, who died in 1518. It was the Agincourt Babington who was largely responsible for the building of the present church. He was also the great grandfather of Anthony Babington, who was beheaded for his part in the Babington Plot to rescue Mary Queen of Scots from Wingfield Manor.

The board also tells a story about Job Wall, the landlord of the inn during the Civil War. A group of Royalists had consumed a large quantity of ale, and Job told them they had had enough. The troops didn't approve of this, and so threw Job Wall out; they drained the inn by consuming as much as they could and wasting the rest.

The area has other events concerned with the Civil War. Eddlestowe Farmhouse was garrisoned in 1644 by a troop of Royalist Dragoons. Eastwood Hall is now in ruins — it was largely blown up by the Parliamentarians in 1646.

THE GREYHOUND INN, ASHOVER — There are several Greyhound Inns in Derbyshire, such as at Dronfield, Kniveton and Ripley. This one dates back to the 17th Century, and was formerly named after a greyhound called The Nettle. Following the dog winning a coursing event, the inn was called, Well Run Nettle. In olden days the Magistrates, William Milnes, of nearby Stubben Edge, held his court in the inn.

ASHFORD IN THE WATER

BULL'S HEAD, ASHFORD IN THE WATER — former coaching inn.

BAKEWELL

CASTLE HOTEL, BAKEWELL — Known originally as the Castle and Commercial Hotel. In front was held the Horse Market. The horses were exercised along New Street.

MANNER'S, BAKEWELL — A former coaching inn with a slanting floor. The inn is named after Sir John Manners, the Marquis of Granby. He commanded the Blues at Minden in 1759, during the 7 year war. Afterwards he set up several soldiers as inn-keepers. See the Marquis of Granby, Bamford, for further details.

QUEEN'S ARMS HOTEL, BRIDGE STREET, BAKEWELL — Georgian building, which was at one time known as The Durham Ox.

THE RED LION, BAKEWELL — The oldest pub in Bakewell, built in 1556. In recent times the inn has been extensively altered internally.

RUTLAND ARMS, RUTLAND SQUARE, BAKEWELL — Bakewell was and still is an important road junction. Evidence still remains of packhorse bridges and turnpike roads. Prior to the beginning of the 19th Century, the site of the Rutland Arms was occupied by the White Horse Inn, a renowned coaching inn and the meeting-place of the Bakewell Rioters in the 18th Century. The inn covered an area of a third of an acre. In 1804 the Rutland Arms was built. William Greaves, a future landlord, was born in the inn in 1807. He eventually became the landlord for fifty years, during which time he took an active part in the town's activities. Among posts he held were Postmaster and A Contractor for the Queen's Highway, which meant running twenty coaches. The stable buildings are across the road. In 1811 Jane Austen stayed here, and her bedroom still exists. In her novel, Pride and Prejudice, one of the meetings between Elizabeth Bennett and Bingley is set in the hotel. In 1790 the 5th Lord Torrington toured Derbyshire, and commented about his stay at the White Horse Inn as follows:

> "I was never in a nastier house. I often arose from my very bad bed to look at the weather, very rainy, a gloomy black morning, all the hills covered by thick mists. Master or Mistress not to be seen having probably been drunk over night."

Perhaps the most important thing that has immortalised Bakewell ever since — the Bakewell Pudding — happened in the inn in about 1859. Mrs. Greaves, the wife of William Greaves, instructed the cook to make a pudding for a special dinner to be held that night. She explained that the egg mixture should be stirred onto the pastry and the strawberry jam spread on top. Somehow the cook forgot the sequence, and put the jam on first and the egg mixture on top. The diners described it as "a delicious pudding".

BAMFORD

LADYBOWER INN, Nr. Ladybower Reservoir, Bamford. — The inn dates from 1821 but before this it had been a sheep farm and known to have existed in the mid-sixteenth century. To the rear of the inn prize fights were held in the 19th century. The inn sign of the reservoir and Lancaster bomber is a tribute to Guy Gibson's 617 Squadron. For eight weeks in 1943 they practised in the Derwent valley, on Derwent Dam, their bombing run using the famous Barnes Wallace bouncing bomb in preparation for the daring mission — The Dambusters — on the night of May 16–17 1943. Sir Barnes Wallace was born in Ripley in Derbyshire. The raid was a great success although only 11 planes returned out of 19. On May 16th 1977 on the 34th anniversary of the raid the last operational Lancaster bomber made its last run, just sixty feet above the water, as on the actual raid of the Ruhr dams.

MARQUIS OF GRANBY HOTEL, BAMFORD — The inn signboard is a painting of John Manners (1721–1770). The Manners home is Haddon Hall, and the wood above the Hall is named Manners Wood. From the early 1700s the Manners rarely resided at Haddon Hall, and instead Belvoir Castle in Leicestershire became the family seat. The legend of Dorothy Vernon, who 'eloped' with (another) John Manners in the 16th Century from Haddon Hall is one of the most famous tales of Derbyshire. Haddon Hall slowly decayed, and it was not until the beginning of this century that the then Marquis of Granby, later to become the ninth Duke of Rutland, took an active interest in the Hall and restored it back to its former glory. John Manners was an English soldier who distinguished himself in the Seven Years War — 1756–63. The Olympic Bar is panelled in oak from the first-class dining cabin of the Olympic, sister ship of the ill-fated Titanic.

THE YORKSHIRE BRIDGE INN, BAMFORD — The inn lies over a mile north of Bamford, close to the dam wall of Ladybower Reservoir. The building dates from 1826. The surrounding houses are more recent, being built to house many of the people who lived in the now submerged villages of Derwent and Ashopton. The Ladybower Reservoir was completed in 1945. The name of the inn comes from the bridge over the River Derwent, just down from the inn at G.R. 198850, and marked on the maps as the Yorkshire Bridge. It was on a packhorse route from Hope Cross and on to Stanage Edge and Sheffield. At first there was a wooden bridge, and in 1695 a stone one was built.

BARLBOROUGH

DE-RODES ARMS, BARLBOROUGH — A very popular inn for the 'post-chase' and stage coaches. Sixteen changes of horses were always at hand. The inn takes its name from the Rodes family, and it was Francis Rodes in 1583 who built the nearby Elizabethan, Barlborough Hall.

BASLOW

THE CAVENDISH HOTEL, BASLOW — Until quite recently this was the Peacock Inn, which had the unique situation of being named after the Dukes of Rutland — the peacock being part of their crest — while being part of the Chatsworth estate. The building has recently been extensively enlarged, and the decor has been under the personal supervision of the Duchess of Devonshire. The end result is a very tasteful and attractive hotel. The name has been changed to the Cavendish, and the emblem is a snake — Serpent nowed proper. The Cavendish family became the Earl of Devonshire in the 17th Century, and later that century

DUKE OF DEVONSHIRE, BELPER    RAILWAY TAVERN, BELPER

DRUID INN, BIRCHOVER    RED LION INN, BIRCHOVER

became the first Duke of Devonshire, whose home, and subsequent Dukes', has been Chatsworth House.

ROBIN HOOD INN, NR. BASLOW. G.R. 279722 — Built in more recent times, the inn is popular with rock climbers who climb on Birchen Edge nearby. There is a Hikers Bar and a small golf course at the rear of the building. Hathersage is Little John country, with his grave in Hathersage Churchyard. In the surrounding area of Hathersage, Baslow and Bakewell are several places christened Robin Hood. For instance, Robin Hood's Cave on Stanage Edge (SK245805); Robin's Hood Cross near Bradwell (SK182803); a chasm at Chatsworth is known as Robin Hood's Leap; Robin Hood's Stoop near Hathersage (SK217806); and Robin Hood's Stride near Winster (SK223623). It is only right that an inn should be named after such a likeable outlaw. Sherwood Forest is not far away, and he certainly came into Derbyshire; in the south of the county, at Doveridge Church, he is said to have been married to Maid Marion under the 1,400-year-old yew tree.

BEELEY

DEVONSHIRE ARMS, BEELEY — The inn dates back to the 17th Century, and is situated in a beautiful village off the B6012 road. Many of the buildings date from the early 19th Century and were designed by Joseph Paxton, the 6th Duke of Devonshire's Head Gardener and friend.

BELPER

KING'S HEAD, BELPER — early 18th century building.

LION HOTEL, BRIDGE STREET, BELPER — A coaching inn dating back to the late 18th century.

TALBOT HOTEL, BRIDGE FOOT, BELPER — One of the oldest inns in Belper; much older than the date stone 1867 suggests. Grade 11 listed building.

OTHER INNS IN BELPER — Along the main street — A6 road — through Belper are a whole string of inns, including The Rifleman's Arms, The Duke of Devonshire, and Lord Nelson. Two others in Belper are the Railway Tavern and the Imperial Vaults. Before Strutt's Mill the main industry was nailmaking. In the early 1800s there were about 10,000 people employed in making nails. Today, apart from one nailmaker's workshop, the industry has gone. The Court Records are full of accounts of the hard drinking nailers. They worked hard up to Friday night then revelled all weekend. Monday was known as Saint Monday so they could recuperate from the weekend!

BIRCHVALE

THE WALTZING WEASEL, BIRCH VALE, NR STOCKPORT — Dates from the 17th Century, and was formerly a principal halt for travellers from the High Peak bound for Stockport and Manchester markets.

BIRCHOVER

DRUID INN, BIRCHOVER — The inn is some 500 years old and takes its name from a religious group, the Druidical, who worshipped on Rowter Rocks behind the inn. The name

Rowter is believed to originate from the local verb 'roo', meaning 'to sway'. There is a rocking stone amongst the stones. These rocks, which can be reached by a path on the far left-hand side of the inn, have passageways, seats, caves, a dungeon and stone armchairs. They were carved in the late 17th and early 18th Century by a member of the Eyre family, who lived nearby.

RED LION INN, BIRCHOVER — A very popular inn in the centre of Birchover village. Inside is an unusual feature — a well in the bar. A glass top and light allow you to look down the deep circular hole.

BOLSOVER

CASTLE INN, BOLSOVER — Built in 1812 as a retirement home for Peter Fiddler, a surveyor and explorer for the Hudson Bay Company, Canada. The building cost 408 1s and 1/2d and took 148 days to construct. After his death a nephew converted it to a beer house and in 1889 was sold to Brampton Brewery Company.

WHITE SWAN, MARKET PLACE, BOLSOVER — Rebuilt in 1915. The orginal inn was used as a mediaeval court.

BONSALL

THE KING'S HEAD, BONSALL — Located opposite one of the most impressive village crosses in Britain. The cross has thirteen steps and was built in 1671. The King's Head was built soon after in 1677, and is a beautiful mullioned window building. A beam in the bar has the following inscription — 1677 Anthony Abell. The prosperity of the village began with lead mining, and in the late 18th Century the population was employed in cotton spinning at Sir Richard Arkwright's mills at Cromford.

PIG OF LEAD, BONSALL — Formerly the inn was known as Via Gellia Inn. Via Gellia gets its name from Philip Gell, who made the road through the wooded gorge from his lead mines to the Cromford Canal in 1791–2. The surrounding area was originally a principal lead-mining area, and opposite the inn is the location of Ball Eye Mine (G.R. 287574). The lead ore extracted here is said to have had the highest content in silver in Derbyshire — as much as twenty ounces of silver per ton.

The name Pig of Lead is from the lead-mining days, when a pig was referred to as a block of cast lead from the smelters works. Eight pigs make one fother. A fother is generally accepted as the weight varying from 1,680 lbs. to 2,520 lbs. A pig of lead was therefore about 210 lbs. to 315 lbs.

BORROWASH

WILMOT ARMS, BORROWASH — 17th Century coaching house, including a malt house. The Wilmot family home was Chaddesden Hall, which has now been demolished, although part of their park still remains.

BRADWELL

SHOULDER OF MUTTON — BRADWELL — Built in the 1930s and takes its name from an earlier inn situated opposite and now a cafe.

BRAILSFORD

THE ROSE AND CROWN, BRAILSFORD — A popular overnight halt for cattle drovers, it was formerly a farm with a licence.

BRASSINGTON

YE OLDE GATE INN — Brassington. — A former coaching inn built in 1616. Brassington was on the King's Highway and mentioned in 1663. John Ogilby's strip maps of 1675 clearly show Brassington on the Manchester to Derby Road. The route was popular although hilly. Defoe in 1727 found the section from Brassington to Buxton — smooth green riding. In 1744 The Duke of Egmont travelled this way in his private coach and found, all the road entirely bad. It had taken him more than five hours to travel the sixteen miles from Derby to Brassington. By the end of the 18th Century the route via Brassington was little used, as Ashbourne became the main overnight halt, although a longer route to Manchester.

In the inn's bar is a small window which opens outwards. The innkeeper would place a mug of ale on the end of a long pole and pass it out to the coachman. Highwaymen waited here for the Post coach and they would hear the post horn when the coach gained the nearby Longcliffe cross roads. Brassington was also a major lead mining area and mine workings are believed to lie beneath the inn. Years ago the miners could be heard working below. The oak panelling in the Dining Room was formerly in the village church.

BRETTON

THE BARREL INN, BRETTON. G.R. 201779. — The highest inn in Derbyshire at 1,240 feet. The view from here over the limestone countryside around Eyam and Foolow is unequalled; on really good days five counties can be seen. The building dates from 1637, and the sign depicts a well-satisfied drinker patting his barrel stomach.

In the entrance are details of people who died here from the bubonic plague that ravished Eyam, in the 17th Century. There are also details of the travels of John Wesley to Eyam woodlands in 1765 during a snowstorm. The inn stands on the line of a Roman road, and it is believed that a house of refreshment has stood here since Roman times.

BROUGH

TRAVELLER'S REST, MAIN ROAD, BROUGH — Former coaching inn on the route to Castleton and Chapel en le Frith. Said to be haunted by a Grey Lady.

BUXTON

BULL I' TH' THORN, on the A515, approximately 6 miles south of BUXTON. G.R. 128665. Beside a Roman Road — The Street — a farm is known to have been here 700 years ago. In 1472 it became known as The Bull, a hostelry. In 1654 it was renamed Hurdlow House and a combination of these names results in todays name. Inside is Tudor pannelling bearing the dates 1642 and 1742. In the 18th century it was a popular coaching inn. The interior contains a wealth of fascinating items including an oak carving of a bull tangled in a thorn bush.

THE CAT AND FIDDLE INN, Nr. BUXTON. G.R. 002719. Although just outside the Derbyshire boundary but within the boundaries of the Peak District National Park, I feel it would be wrong to omit such an historic inn, and the second highest inn in the country at 1,690 feet above sea level. For more than 200 years roads have passed the front door of the inn. Near the inn on an old turnpike road can be found a milestone — To London 164 miles. In 1831 the Cat & Fiddle Inn was described by a traveller — A newly erected and well accustomed inn or public house. It was built by John Ryle, a Macclesfield banker. How the inn came to be named the Cat and Fiddle is still a mystery, but perhaps the following legend has a hint of truth about it.

Wherefore Cat? and why Fiddle?
Pray solve me the riddle.
The Air makes one dance,
Without Fiddle we prance.

Oer the moorland and heather,
In the best of all weather,
In the brave days of old
(So I was yesterday told),
We, as usual, were warring with France,
And Calais had taken by chance.

A worthy Knight Caton by name,
For England's King then held the same,
The French unable to turn him out,
Caton le Fidele would frequently shout.

Now with this Knight a country wight,
Had fought with all his main and might,
The war was o'er, and in Buxton town
This country wight had settled down.

A hillside man, fond of fresh air,
A house then built, the prospect fair,
For sale of ale, and wine, and mead,
And wondrously he did succeed.

The house he built had yet no name,
Although his house increased in fame.
Mine host would talk of fights and France,
While his cronies many a name advance.

He dreamed one night of that daunty Knight,
Caton le Fidele and of many a fight.
Then waking said, His name I give
My House — Caton Fidele — while I live.

The country folk were puzzled sore,
The name they read it o'er and o'er.
At length they said, Heigh! diddle, diddle,
Why sure it must be Cat and Fiddle!

Another suggestion as to how it was named. The sixth Duke of Devonshire gave the Landlord in 1857 a photograph of a cat and fiddle.

CAT AND FIDDLE, NR BUXTON

BULL I' TH' THORN, NR BUXTON

THE OLD HALL HOTEL, THE CRESCENT, BUXTON — Mary Queen of Scots was 'imprisoned' in Derbyshire for seventeen years, 1569-1587. During most of this time her 'gaoler' was the 6th Earl of Shrewsbury, George Talbot. He had numerous estates in Derbyshire, such as Chatsworth, Sheffield Castle and Tutbury Castle just in Staffordshire. In the 1570s he was improving Buxton Hall, now the Old Hall Hotel, and the oldest building in Lower Buxton. Mary wanted to go to Bwkstons Well for a few days, and finally went in the summer of 1573, staying there at the Buxton Hall. The last time she was there was in 1584, and before she left she scratched on a window pane of the Hall –

> Buxton, whose fame thy milk-warm waters tell,
> Whom I, perhaps, no more shall see, farewell!

The present building dates from 1670 and has a five-bay front and a door on Tuscan pillars.

THE CHESHIRE CHEESE INN, 41 HIGH STREET, BUXTON — Dates from the 18th century; in 1787 S.W.Ryley treated an actor friend to a trout supper here. In 1811 the owner and licensee was Mrs Ann Mycock and in 1846 the landlord was Solomon Mycock. His christian name is used for the temple he built in 1896, using unemployed people, on the summit of Grin Low above Poole Cavern. In the 19th century the inn had a bowling green, the only one in Buxton.

THE SUN INN, 35 HIGH STREET, BUXTON — In 1837 the inn was known as the Rising Sun but by 1841 was known as The Sun, and has remained so ever since. For much of the 19th century the inn was owned and run by the Bennett family. The area around here including the Market and St. Anne's Church is the original part of Buxton known as Higher Buxton. The newer part — Lower Buxton — is situated around The Crescent. In November 1577, Higher Buxton consisted of about fifty houses with two inns and eight alehouses, catering basically for visitors and travellers. At this time it was the only place in the High Peak to have an inn.

OLD SWAN INN, HIGH STREET, BUXTON — Dates from the 17th Century and a former brewery.

THE KINGS HEAD HOTEL, BUXTON — the history of the building, which was once a Manse, is recorded in a frame in the lounge bar. In the late 18th Century the Minister preferred to stay in a nearby house that he rented. He let the Manse as an inn in about 1784.

C

CASTLETON

BULL'S HEAD HOTEL, CASTLETON — said to have a secret passage leading to Peveril Castle.

THE CASTLE HOTEL, CASTLETON — A haunted hostelry. On many occasions a white lady has been seen flitting through the passageways. She is believed to be a jilted lover whose husband-to-be did not turn up at the church at the appointed hour. In fact he was never seen. They were to have had a wedding breakfast at the hotel. She died broken-hearted, and periodically walks into the dining room where they were to have eaten. She has not been seen for a long time, but another ghost was seen by the landlord in 1960. A man in a blue pin-stripe suit disappeared into thin air. Under one of the stone steps is reputed to be the body of a murdered woman, placed there in 1603.

YE OLDE NAG'S HEAD, CASTLETON — A coaching inn dating back to the 17th Century. Castleton was a major coaching halt on the Sheffield-Manchester turnpike road. At the beginning of the 19th Century Pickfords operated a wagon service to Manchester. The 16 miles from Sheffield to Castleton took 8 hours.

CHAPEL EN LE FRITH

THE DOG INN, MARKET STREET, CHAPEL EN LE FRITH — The original inn was next door, and the present location was formerly a grocer's shop. Its original name was Talbot, named after the dog, which no longer exists today, that was trained to run between three pairs of horses pulling the Earl of Shrewsbury's carriage. The sixth Earl of Shrewsbury, who owned considerable estates in Derbyshire and was Mary Queen of Scots gaoler, was Sir George Talbot. Hence the name of the dog. Another rare fact about the inn is that it has a Queen Anne's Licence. Very few exist today, and the licence cannot be revoked, except by Act of Parliament.

JOLLY CARTER, BUXTON ROAD, CHAPEL EN LE FRITH — As the inn sign records, the inn was a popular halt for carters who stabled their pack horses here, before traversing the remote moorland routes.

THE ROYAL OAK, MARKET STREET, CHAPEL EN LE FRITH — a former coaching inn. The Peak Ranger coach to Stockport and Manchester departed from here. The inn was also used periodically as the Magistrates' Court. Nearby in the Market Place are the village stocks.

CHESTERFIELD

In the 1880s the following amusing column was printed in the Derbyshire Times on Chesterfield's old public houses:–

> "The other day when walking through the town I was not a little startled by the roaring of the DURHAM OX, and, not liking the look of the HORNS, I beat a hasty retreat into the COMMERCIAL. Having refreshed myself and regained my breath, I returned on my way, when there appeared in my path a BULL'S HEAD of so extraordinary a kind that it was reputed to be near THREE TUNS. It is not often that the stranger can obtain so free an entrance to the presence of RUTLAND or DEVONSHIRE, much less so august a personage as His Highness the PRINCE OF WALES, as he can in Chesterfield, nor, except at the Tower of London, in the regalia room, can the real CROWN AND SCEPTRE be seen for nothing. After seeking spiritual comfort from the OLD ANGEL, the cry of the PEACOCK caused me to turn round, and I noticed a GREEN MAN mounted on a WHITE HORSE, hunting the BUCK under the branches of the ROYAL OAK. Not far distant SHAKESPEARE and BYRON were guiding the PLOUGH through the TURF, when

up came DERBY with his noble VOLUNTEERS, just in time to rescue the CROWN and save the KING'S HEAD, for which service he received the decoration of the STAR AND GARTER. I afterwards visited the THREE HORSE SHOES to join in the debate on FREE TRADE, and, having done so, I heard the BLUE BELL ring violently. On rushing out I found a fight going on between the MINERS and the BRICKMAKERS, who had laid aside their MALLETS AND TOOLS, SQUARE AND COMPASSES, and were at CROSS DAGGERS. There was a general commotion. THE RED LION was roaring at the LEOPARD, the SPREAD EAGLE was pulling the FEATHERS out of the WHITE SWANS, while the HARE AND HOUNDS were chasing the BLACK BULL all round the EXCHANGE. At this time out came the STAR, giving a light almost equal to the SUN, who with DOG AND GUN and BIRD IN HAND and not in the best of humour, left the town clearing the way for the KING AND MILLER, who had just arrived in the OLD SHIP, now laying at ANCHOR near the Spa, making the best of their way to the ANGEL, where I left them with the JUG AND GLASS, leaning against the CROWN AND ANCHOR. The FREEMASONS in their excitement upset the HARE AND GREYHOUND, damaging the WHEATSHEAF, and burying BRITANNIA under the BARLEY MOW, afterwards climbing to the top of the FOUNTAIN and throwing down the WOOLPACK, knocking MILTON'S HEAD right over the CROOKED SPIRE.'

From: T.P. Wood's Almanac 1933.

YE OLDE ANGEL HOTEL, PACKERS ROW, CHESTERFIELD — Once were two inns, the Angel and Star. A principal coaching inn with the Leeds and London Mail coaches calling. Packhorse teams used to rest here on their north to south and Pennine routes. Packers Row records their trade and the nearby shops made saddles and packhorse harnesses.

BLUE STOOPS, CHESTERFIELD — Built late last century; about 1891. The name is derived from two colloquialisms — blue meaning stone and stoops meaning posts. See the Blue Stoops in Dronfield for another version!

YE OLDE CROOKED SPIRE, CHURCH WAY, CHESTERFIELD — It is fitting that one inn should record Chesterfield's finest asset. The spire standing 228 feet high and leaning 8 feet was built at the end of the 14th century. It is believed the spire was constructed from green timbers which on drying out distorted. There are many legends explaining why it is crooked. Several concern the devil who on misdemeanours in Nottingham often flew past. On occasions he alighted on the spire to rest. Once he wrapped his tail round and on leaving pulled the spire! Another story relates how tired he was and one day he bumped into it. Another story relates that the first people to be married in the church were so innocent the spire crooked. It will only return to the vertical when the next innocent couple are married!

GOLDEN FLEECE, KNIFESMITHGATE, CHESTERFIELD — The ceiling rafters in the Tudor Bar came from Bolsover Castle in 1762.

MARKET HOTEL, MARKET PLACE, CHESTERFIELD — Overlooking the Market area and its licence dates back to 1720.

THE PEACOCK INN, 67 LOW PAVEMENT, CHESTERFIELD — No longer an inn, but the building, which has a splendid wooden facade, remains. In the 1970s the site was excavated, and the finds gave a fascinating insight into mediaeval Chesterfield. The building has been carefully restored, and is now known as The Peacock Centre, with Information Office and Heritage Centre. To the rear can be seen the inn sign letters.

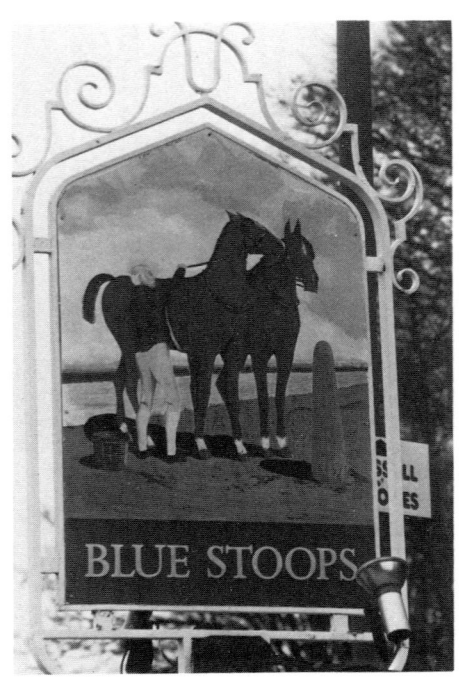

BLUE STOOPS, CHESTERFIELD

YE OLDE CROOKED SPIRE INN, CHESTERFIELD

THE MARKET INN, CHESTERFIELD

THE ROYAL OAK, CHESTERFIELD

PORTLAND HOTEL, CHESTERFIELD — Built about 1898 upon the site of the Bird in Hand Inn, which was demolished in the late 1890s. The Dukes of Portland used to own Bolsover Castle.

THE ROYAL OAK, SHAMBLES, CHESTERFIELD — Formerly the rest house of the Knights Templars, who after the Crusades settled at nearby Temple Normanton. There they planted a damson tree brought back from the Holy Land. The first recorded Deed to the premises is dated 1684, when a plot of land was sold to build an extension to the Royal Oak. The Shambles was a Butchers' Market, and two butchers' shops are incorporated into the inn. In 1897 Stones Brewery Company of Sheffield took over the inn and carried out restoration work. Wood from a derelict building below the Durham Ox in Irongate was used. Today it is a magnificent half-timbered building.

WELBECK INN, SORESBY STREET, CHESTERFIELD — Dates from the 17th Century and must be the most changed-named inn in Chesterfield. It was first known as the Three Cranes; in the 1800's as the Tiger Inn then Dyson's Vaults and since the end of last century as the Welbeck Inn.

CHINLEY

OLD HALL INN, CHINLEY — Former 14th century Manor House with a secret passageway to the church.

CHINLEY HEAD

LAMB INN, CHINLEY HEAD, NR HAYFIELD — Built in 1769, and the Licence dating from this time still survives.

CLAY CROSS

GEORGE & DRAGON, 175, High Street, Clay Cross. — The Derbyshire Courier, dated February 12th 1842, records the occasion when an Inquest was held at the inn, with Mr J. Hutchinson as Coroner. The verdict of the jury on the death of Mrs Elizabeth Wetherall, aged 23, was 'died by the visitation of God.' Her husband, a collier, sold all the furniture in their house and spent the money on drink. This resulted in Elizabeth sleeping on a bed of straw and having no food to eat for two weeks before her death, except for an occasional drink given by neighbours. The surgeon from Ashover, Mr Macarsie, who performed a post mortem confirmed that she had starved to death. Although her husband was taken into custody no charges were brought as there was no proof of violence. Their child died two weeks before her mother's death, having been poisoned by a neighbour with an overdose of laudanum (tincture of opium). Following his discharge, Mr. Wetherall left Clay Cross with another woman!

During alterations in 1985, the landlord, Mr D. Fowler, found two Bills of Sale for blasting powder dated 1858 and a legal letter dated the same year. The latter was addressed to Richard Clarke to pay overdue rent of 9 old pence, in lieu of tithes on land he occupied in the parish. The money was to be paid to Joseph Gratton on Friday, 29th January 1858, between the hours of 10 and 12 at the George & Dragon Inn in Clay Cross.

BEE HIVE INN, COMBS

THE ABBEY, DARLEY ABBEY

GREYHOUND INN, CROMFORD

CLIFTON

COCK INN, CLIFTON, NR. ASHBOURNE — Dates back to about 1500 A.D. The name Cock is a reminder of those days when cock-fighting was a popular sport.

COMBS

THE OLD BEE HIVE INN, COMBS — The present inn was built in 1863. The original inn stood on the former road to Chapel-en-le-Frith via Dane Hey and Combs Meadows, and was at right angles to its present position on the Green. Part of the decoration inside is a collection of chamber pots hanging from the ceiling.

HANGING GATE INN, COMBS — The inn sign is a gate bearing the words — This gate hangs free and hinders none.
Refresh yourself and travel on.

CRICH

THE JOVIAL DUTCHMAN INN, CRICH — A delightful name for an inn, but as to how it became so named I cannot discover. In 1915 it was described as a modern hotel having apartments and board residence with horse and pony turnouts for hire. Visitors met at all stations — five minutes from the famous stand.

CROMFORD

THE GREYHOUND HOTEL, CROMFORD — Cromford is immortalised by the 'genius' of Sir Richard Arkwright, who started the first water-powered spinning mill here in 1769. The inn was built by him in 1788, and the frontage, of splendid Georgian workmanship, has remained unaltered for almost 200 years. In 1790 Arkwright obtained permission to hold a market at Cromford. At the end of Market Day the following poem was pinned to the inn door.

> Come let us all here join in one,
> And thank him for all favours done;
> Let's thank him for all favours still
> Which he hath done besides the mill.
>
> Modistly drink liquor about,
> And see whose health you can find out;
> This one I chuse before the rest
> Sir Richard Arkwright is the best.
>
> A few more words I have to say
> Success to Cromford's market day.

On the right of the inn, on "Scarthin", is another inn, named The Boat Inn, which was built in 1772.

CROWDICOTE

THE PACKHORSE INN, CROWDICOTE. G.R. 101652. — Situated right on the Derbyshire/Staffordshire boundary beside the River Dove. As the name suggests, Crowdicote was on a packhorse route to Longnor. During those days the inn was in the adjacent building. A stone packhorse bridge was built here in 1709; prior to that there was a wooden footbridge. The name Crowdicote is said to derive from Crawdy Coat Bridge. In the Domesday Book it is mentioned as Cruda's Cot. Cruda, a Saxon, owned this area.

CUBLEY

HOWARD ARMS, GREAT CUBLEY — Known locally as the Cubley Stoop. The stoop is a block of mounting steps for ladies to mount their horse, side saddle, and is by the stables at the rear of the building.

D

DARLEY ABBEY

THE ABBEY, DARLEY ABBEY — Originally part of a 12th Century Augustine Priory that was founded here in 1137. Many of the buildings were demolished in Henry V111's reign. The building dates from the 15th century and has been beautifully restored, winning a conservation award.

DARLEY BRIDGE

SQUARE AND COMPASS INN, DARLEY BRIDGE — Built in 1735. On the roadside wall is a parish boundary stone — North Darley/South Darley.

THREE STAGS HEAD, DARLEY BRIDGE — 18th century inn. Above the main doorway is the date and owner's initials — 17 G.O.Q. 36.

DARLEY DALE

THE WHITWORTH HOTEL, DARLEY DALE — Located at the junction of the B5057 and A6 roads. The Park and Institute buildings were built by Sir Joseph Whitworth, designed by Oliver and Atcherley of Manchester, and opened in 1890. Originally they formed part of a large plan, but only half the buildings were built. The Whitworth Hotel was originally the schoolmaster's home. Sir Joseph Whitworth was born in Stockport in 1803. From 1840 onwards he began working on a standard of measuring. He also designed machinery, and invented the Whitworth rifle. His connection with Darley Dale spans several years, for he lived for fifteen years at Stancliffe Hall, now a Boys' Preparatory School, and took an active interest in local affairs. He was created a baronet in 1869 and died in 1887.

MR. JORROCKS, DERBY    OLDE DOLPHIN INN, DERBY

SEVEN STARS INN, DERBY

26

DERBY

BELL HOTEL, SADLER GATE, DERBY — Former 18th century coaching inn known until 1771 as the Bell and Castle. Here the famous Derby Fly stopped overnight before heading on for London. The half timbered facade was added in 1929. Viscount Torrington stayed here in 1789 and described the inn — as good an Inn as can be found amongst the bad ones in the town.

THE BELL AND CASTLE INN, BURTON ROAD, DERBY — Formerly an 18th century stockinger's cottage. The long windows at the back allow daylight through for the frames in front of them. In the late 18th Century there were more then 4,000 stockingers in Derby. They worked a 15 hour day for very little money, which lead to rioting. The inn was listed in 1796 and was originally one cottage with the landlord living next door. In 1910 the adjacent cottage was converted to a bar, another in 1955 and a fourth in 1981. The three storeyed building still has the original beams, although warped, and the inner walls are wattle and daub. A previous landlady collected bells and there are now more than 200 of them from 26 countries. They include a Derby Town Crier's bell, a train bell, a fire engine bell and a ship's bell. Of pasrticular note is the Handyside Foundary works bell, situated in Duke Street, Derby from 1810–1912. The bell was rung when work was available and could be heard as far as Little Eaton. The bell was also rung when iron bars were in production. Previous owners are convinced that a ghost haunts the building.

THE BROADWAY, DUFFIELD ROAD, DERBY — Formerly a large private house, but in 1936 was converted to an inn.

DUKE OF CLARENCE, MANSFIELD ROAD, DERBY — Originally a farmhouse and in the 19th Century a coaching inn. Derby's only well dressing custom takes place close by.

DOLPHIN INN, QUEEN STREET, DERBY — The oldest inn in Derby being built in the same year as the cathedral tower, 1530. Grade 11 listed building.

EXETER ARMS, EXETER PLACE, DERBY — The last place in Derby where house brewed ale was made, finishing in 1969.

THE FRIARY HOTEL, FRIAR GATE, DERBY — The hotel was built as a private house in about 1710. The name derives from the fact that the building is on the site of a monastery built in the 10th Century, and was a home of the Blackfriars. In 1900 the private house was converted to an hotel. There are tales of a ghost — a hooded monk — walking the passageways, but nothing conclusive has been substantiated. The rooms reflect the history of the site — The Benedictine Suite and the Monks Retreat.

MR JORROCKS, IRONGATE, DERBY — Formerly known as The Globe.

THE MAYPOLE INN, LITTLEOVER, DERBY — Victorian building opened in about 1874. Inside the landlord's collection of fishing rods has been used to make an unusual ceiling decoration, including a harpoon.

YE OLDE SPA INN, ABBEY STREET, DERBY — Built in 1773 by a Mr Chambers. The murderer, Richard Thorley, had his last drink of freedom here before being arrested. He was later hanged in Derby in 1862; the last public execution in Derby.

THE SEVEN STARS, KING STREET, DERBY. Built in 1680 it is Derby's second oldest inn and stands on the site of an early Augustine Monastery. Formerly known as The Plough as recorded in William Hutton's, History of Derby, in 1791. It is believed the present name derives from the Plough star sign of seven stars. From 1680 to 1962 beer was brewed on the premises. During alterations in the 1960s a 27 foot deep well was found in the former kitchen and the pure water is believed to have been used in the brewing. At one time tankards made by the then nearby Crown Derby factory were used to serve the ale.

Although never a coaching inn it is evident from the cobbled yard and stabling that passing traffic formed part of its trade. The Derby to Rugeley horse-drawn mail coaches frequently called. Over the years the inn has seen many characters. One was Dick Oliver with a highly coloured nose. Another was a landlord who judged the stability of his customers by the way they negotiated the tricky doorstep. The present owner informs me they have a resident ghost called George.

OLD SILK MILL, DERBY — The mural on the outside wall recalls much of the history of the area. John Lambe, whose silk mill (now the Derby Industrial Museum) is close by, committed the first act of industrial espionage by stealing Piedmont designs. He was later poisoned. The mural deals with the historic Derby Turnout on 1833 and struggle in 1834 when mill workers fought for the right to combine.

WARDWICK TAVERN, THE WARDWICK, DERBY — 18th century coaching inn with coach entrance. The building is a Grade 11 listed building.

DETHICK

WHITE HART INN, MOORWOOD MOOR, NR. DETHICK — Former coaching inn dating back to the 16th Century. The stables have now been incorporated into the inn and are now a bar.

DRONFIELD

THE BLUE STOOPS, HIGH STREET, DRONFIELD — The building dates from the 16th Century, and two date stones with the date 1596 can be seen — one on the front of the building, and the other on the fireplace in the righthand bar. The building was rebuilt in the 18th Century. The cellars are partly hewn out of the bedrock. The origin of the inn name is not fully understood. Originally the inn was named Blue Posts, and may possibly derive from the custom of painting the door posts a specific colour to indicate an inn. In the late 19th Century the inn sign depicted two stoops, barring entry to cars into a yard.

THE GREEN DRAGON, DRONFIELD — The present three-storeyed inn with mullioned windows was rebuilt in the early 17th Century, but the origins date back to the 14th Century. The inn is opposite the parish church, dedicated to St. John the Baptist. It is believed that the inn was the residence of Chantry priests, who duty was to pray for the dead in the church. Inside the church is a unique brass to two chantry priests, the Gomfrey brothers. Richard

GREEN DRAGON INN, DRONFIELD

KING'S HEAD, DUFFIELD

THE QUIET WOMAN, EARL STERNDALE

BULLS HEAD, EYAM

Gomfrey was a Chantry priest from 1367 to 1380. In 1349, the Guild of the Blessed Virgin Mary was endowed and the building was their headquarters. It seems probable that the inn came into being in Henry VIII's reign, when guilds and chantrys were dissolved. In the left hand bar the wall is also part of the adjoining Chantry Hotel that dates back to 1300. In this party wall is a mediaeval archway.

THE HYDE PARK INN, HILLTOP, DRONFIELD — About 100 years old. The original owner, who happened to be in Hyde Park in London when he first learned that a licence had been granted, decided to call the inn The Hyde Park.

THE WHITE SWAN, DRONFIELD — In a lease dated 1678 the building is described for the first time. It was not until 1722 that the building was first mentioned as an inn. It was sold for 14 to George Taylor of Dronfield, Innkeeper, by Francis Burton, a former Lord of the Manor. Half a mile towards Sheffield on the A61 is Rock Tavern. A datestone on the building is IC 1677.

DUFFIELD

KING'S HEAD, DUFFIELD — Dates from the mid-16th Century, is on two levels and has 3' thick walls. From Cromwellian days the inn has been used as a billet by soldiers. The last occasion was in the 1880s, when it was used as an Officers' Mess. In 1787/88 the first Land Commission used the inn as their base for sharing out the surrounding common land.

PATTERNMAKERS ARMS, DUFFIELD — Victorian inn named after patternmakers who made clogs.

E

EARL STERNDALE

THE QUIET WOMAN, EARL STERNDALE. G.R. 090670. — The sign depicts a headless woman with the words — Soft words turneth away wrath. How the inn came to be so named is a mystery, but two stories are told as possible explanations.

One states that the landlady was a constant chatterbox, and the older she became the more she talked. Late in life she began talking in her sleep as well. By this time the long-suffering landlord and villagers had had enough. The only course of action left was to remove her head, as the inn sign depicts! The villagers gave the landlord permission, and he did the deed. Peace once more reigned over the village. It is said that a tombstone was erected in the graveyard and the epitaph was a warning to other chatterboxes.

The other tale. The landlord always went to Longnor Market, 2 miles away, every week. He was a man of habit and always returned home at the same time, but on one occasion he was delayed and did not reach home until late at night. His wife was angry that he was late, and he was likewise angry at her unreasonable behaviour and for sending someone to look for him.

They argued with neither party giving in. Finally the landlord walked out and said, If I can't have a quiet woman inside, I will have a quiet woman outside. He instructed the inn sign to be painted!

EDALE

OLD NAG'S HEAD — EDALE — The final watering hole before setting off up the Pennine Way, via Grindsbrook. As the inns name recalls, the inn was also a major stopping point for packhorse teams on their way from Yorkshire to Lancashire carrying wool and stone. The inn dates from 1576.

THE RAMBLER INN — EDALE — Built early this century in Victorian railway style and known for many years as the Church Hotel , then Jolly Rambler and now belonging to the Ramblers Holiday concern, "The Rambler".

EDNASTON

YEW TREE INN, EDNASTON — an old inn named after an ancient yew tree which stands beside the inn.

ETWALL

THE SPREAD EAGLE, ETWALL — Built in the 17th Century.

EYAM

BULL'S HEAD HOTEL, EYAM. Opposite the church, and like many of the buildings in Eyam, a small board details the history. On this site in 1606 stood the Talbot Inn. Originally it had a thatched roof, and in about 1710 the name was changed to the Bull's Heade.

MINERS' ARMS, EYAM — The inn was built before the plague, in 1630. The surrounding neighbourhood of Eyam was a major lead-mining area, as the inn sign suggests. North of the village is the site of New Engine Mine. It was operating up to 1884 but is today just a ruin. In 1860 a new shaft was sunk here to a depth of 1,092 feet, making it the deepest lead mine shaft in Derbyshire. Relics of lead mining can be seen inside the inn.

Also in the inn can be seen details of a mock marriage between the rector of Eyam, Joseph Hunt, and the landlord's daughter Anne. The occasion happened in 1684.

A stone in the corner of the vestry records the death of Joseph Hunt, Rector of Eyam, who was buried on December 16th, 1709, and of his wife Anne, who died six years previously. She was the daughter of a village publican, whom he had been obliged by the Bishop to marry in consequence of his having gone through a mock ceremony with her in a drunken freak. This caused an action of breach of promise with a Derby lass to whom he was previously engaged. Some years passed in litigation, which drained his purse and estranged his friends; and eventually he had to take shelter in the vestry (which some say was built for that purpose) where he resided for the remainder of his life to keep the law hounds at bay.

F

FLAGG

THE PLOUGH INN, FLAGG — dates from the 18th century.

FOOLOW

THE LAZY LANDLORD, FOOLOW — Formerly known as the Bull's Head Inn. Situated in the peaceful and attractive village of Foolow, overlooking the green and village pond. The nearby cross dates from the 14th century and was placed here in 1868. Beside it is a bull ring, one of the few to be seen in Derbyshire.

FROGGATT EDGE

THE CHEQUERS INN, FROGGATT EDGE — Built between 1550-1600 by the Hallam family of Calver on land owned by the Duke of Rutland and beside an old packhorse route. Named the Chequers because the local overseer used to sit here and collect the rates from the villagers. Those who could not afford to pay would be set to work as stone-masons in the nearby quarries. The chequers sign is reputed to be the world's oldest. A slab marked into squares like a chess board was originally the mark of a wine shop 2,000 years ago.

The inn was rebuilt in 1735. It is said the Eyam body-snatchers in the 18th century called here for refreshemnt en route for Sheffield cemetery. The infamous Guy Fawkes is reputed to be buried nearby.

FENNY BENTLEY

COACH AND HORSES INN, FENNY BENTLEY — As the name suggests, it was on a coaching route; the building dates from the 17th Century.

FURNESS VALE

SOLDIER DICK, FURNESS VALE — The unusual name refers to an older coaching inn where an army deserter was secretly hidden away. He spent his time painting and these are now in Chester Museum.

G

GLAPWELL

YOUNG VANISH INN, GLAPWELL, NR CHESTERFIELD — The inn was formerly known as the Gardeners Arms. However, the landlord won a great deal of money on the racehorse known as The Young Vanish, and as a result changed the inn's name.

GLOSSOP

THE GROUSE INN, CHUNAL ROAD, GLOSSOP — Formerly a 17th Century farmhouse.

GREAT LONGSTONE

CRISPIN INN, GREAT LONGSTONE — dates from the early 17th Century with some parts 18th Century. Completely remodernised in 1970.

GRINDLEFORD

THE MAYNARD ARMS HOTEL, GRINDLEFORD — The present inn dates from the beginning of this century; built in 1900. The earlier inn was on the other side of the road. It is named after Sir Richard Lax Maynard who fought in the Battle of Agincourt in 1415. A descendant, Thomas Maynard, was killed at Flodden Field in 1513. Battle scenes, dress and armour are incorporated into the decor of the hotel.

The Maynards are a Yorkshire family and still have descendants living in Pickering in Yorkshire. The Derbyshire connection stems from Edmund Jefferson Maynard, who married, in the late 19th Century, a Sitwell of Stainsby. He owned land in Derbyshire and became Lord of the Manor of Nether Padley.

THE SIR WILLIAM HOTEL, GRINDLEFORD — Controversy surrounds which Sir William the inn refers to. The nearby road and hill are also named Sir William. A guide book to the Peak District in 1899 says — The road which rises in a bee line for one and three quarter miles from a height of 850 feet .... to 1324 feet may have been named after Sir William Peveril, the natural son of William the Conqueror. Another suggestion is that it refers to Sir William Saville, the second Marquis of Halifax, who in the 17th Century was Lord of Manor of Eyam. The inn sign is a painting of Sir William Bagshawe (1771 – 1832). There is more evidence to suggest that this was the man the road, inn and hill is named after.

The road, although a section over the hill is now just a rough track, was at one time an important road to Tideswell, one of the principal Peak District villages. Sir William Bagshawe had several estates — Oaker Park at Norton, Sheffield; Goosehill Hall and Wormhill Hall. It is said that to help get to his estates quickly he had the road over the hill repaired. A portrait still exists showing Sir William's favourite son sitting on the summit of Sir William Hill. Sir William played an important role in Derbyshire life; in 1805 he was appointed High Sheriff of Derbyshire, and a year later he was knighted.

H

HADFIELD

PEELS ARMS, HADFIELD — A strange custom still survives here, known as holing. There is a hole in the wall, and anyone who can get through it is awarded a certificate.

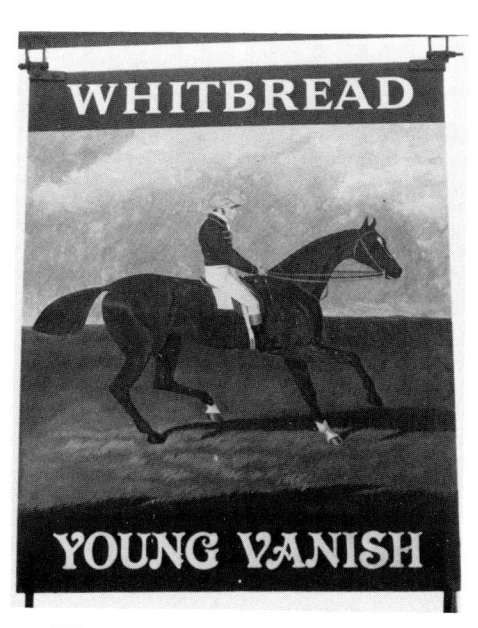

YOUNG VANISH INN, GLAPWELL

LITTLE JOHN INN, HATHERSAGE

SCOTSMAN'S PACK INN, HATHERSAGE

34

HARDSTOFT

THE SHOULDER OF MUTTON INN, HARDSTOFT — A popular inn with extensive function rooms, situated beside a road junction on the B6039 road, near Hardwick Hall. The original part of the complex was a farm dating from 1672.

HARTINGTON

CHARLES COTTON HOTEL, HARTINGTON — Charles Cotton is one of 'Derbyshire's' most famous sons, and was born at Beresford Hall nearby in 1630. The Hall, which is now in ruins with very little remaining to be seen, is in fact on the Staffordshire side of the River Dove, but Derbyshire has poached him! He was a great friend of Izaak Walton, and together they fished the Dove. Charles Cotton's Fishing Temple still exists. Cotton would sit on the steps and smoke a pipeful of tobacco, which he called his breakfast. Cotton wrote several books, including an addition to Izaak Walton's book, The Compleat Angler. The addition on 'Fly Fishing' was included in the 5th edition printed in 1676. The piece was scribbled in ten days. Charles Cotton died in 1687, and a memorial to him is in St. James's Church, Piccadilly.

His companion, Izaak Walton (1593-1683) is remembered by the Izaak Walton Hotel (G.R. 144508) situated at the bottom of Dovedale and just inside Staffordshire.

HASSOP

THE EYRE ARMS, HASSOP, NR. BAKEWELL — There are several Eyre Arms in the area, such as at Calver nearby. This one dates back to the 16th Century and has an interesting collection of antiques inside. The Eyre family have been associated with the Hope Valley area since Norman times. According to tradition, the following explains how they came to this area, how they were named Eyre, and how the Inn sign depicts a single leg above the shield.

During the Battle of Hastings in 1606 a soldier named Truelove found William the Conqueror knocked off his horse, with his helmet restricting his breathing. Truelove helped to remove the helmet. When William could speak he asked Truelove his name. William replied, From now on your name shall be Air, for you have given me air to breathe. A few hours later, William went to see how Air was getting on. William found him injured, and soon afterwards one of his legs had to be amputated. William told Air that he would give him some land when he had recovered from his injury. Air said, I shall call it Hope, for you have given me hope to live.

HATHERSAGE

THE GEORGE HOTEL, HATHERSAGE — Originally a coaching inn built in the 16th Century, but has been extensively modernised. Stage coach travellers stayed at the inn, where the fare and accommodation was primitive. In the early 19th Century it was an eight hour journey from Sheffield through Hathersage to Castleton. In 1845 Charlotte Bronte alighted from a stage coach here to stay at the vicarage. Later, as a result of her visit she wrote Jane Eyre. Hathersage can clearly be seen as Morton in the book. The name Morton was from the surname of the landlord of the George Hotel. Eyre is from the Eyre family who were the main landowners in the area, and Hathersage Church has several excellent brasses to them. Moorseats is Moor House; North Lees Hall is Marsh End; and Fox House is believed to be Whitcross where Jane left the coach on her flight.

THE HATHERSAGE INN, HATHERSAGE — Built in 1808 by Major A.A. Shuttleworth, who had been in the Royal Artillery in the American War of Independence. Originally it was known as the Ordnance Arms. At the rear of the car park can be seen the gig house and stables, whilst at the entrance is the location of the brew house.

LITTLE JOHN HOTEL, HATHERSAGE — It is only natural that an inn in Hathersage should be named after Robin Hood's companion. Derbyshire is Little John country, and the cottage he lived in in Hathersage has long since disappeared. On Longshaw estate is Little John Well, about three miles from Hathersage. In Hathersage churchyard is the tomb to Little John. The title of 'little' seems a misnomer, for when the grave was excavated in 1784, by John Shuttleworth, a thigh bone 29 inches long was found. This would make Little John eight feet tall. The grave is 13 feet long. The inn sign depicts Little John.

"His bow was in the chancel hung;
His last good bolt they drave
Down to the rocks, its measured length
Westward fro' the grave.

And root and bud this shaft put forth
When spring returned anon;
It grew a tree, and threw a shade,
Where slept staunch Little John."

THE MILLSTONE INN, HATHERSAGE. G.R. 242807. — The name is taken from the once active industry that operated along all the gritstone edges of the eastern side of the Peak District, in the 18th and 19th Centuries. Numerous millstones can still be seen on these, especially at Millstone Edge half a mile to the east of the inn. In 1811 a pair of millstones 5 ft. in diameter were sold for 10 guineas (10.50p).

SCOTSMAN'S PACK INN, THE DALE, HATHERSAGE — An inn has occupied this site since the 14th Century. The present building dates from 1912. The inn name is from the Scottish packmen who travelled the packways of England in the 16th and 17th Centuries. A packhorse way goes through Hathersage over Surprise View to Longshaw and Chesterfield. Another goes over Stanedge Pole to Sheffield. Scottish tailors used to sell their suits to farmers on market day in the inn. Inside the inn is Little John's chair. Little John is buried in Hathersage Churchyard. The chair was won in a wager by Major G. Thomas, Manchester Regiment, from Lieutenant A. Sunderland, M.C., Royal Tank Regiment in 1950. It was presented to the Scotsman Pack Inn by Mrs. N. Lucas in October 1960. Opposite the inn is the village pinfold.

HAYFIELD

THE GEORGE HOTEL, HAYFIELD — 16th Century inn originally built as a mail house. Linking the hotel to an old wash house is an underground passage. During the times of chain gang recruitment, people escaped along this tunnel. The first Derby Militia was formed here in 1808.

THE PACK HORSE INN, HAYFIELD — The inn dates back to the 15th Century. Since mediaeval days Hayfield was an important stopping point for packhorse teams right up to the 18th Century. Having crossed the edge of Kinder from the Vale of Edale, via Jacobs Ladder to Edale Cross, Hayfield must have been a welcome sight after crossing such remote countryside.

THE ROYAL HOTEL, HAYFIELD — The building, built in 1755, has had a chequered career. For a while it was the vicarage for the vicar, named Badley. He proved himself very popular, and the deeds, instead of being made out to the vicar of Hayfield, were made out to Badley himself. Upon his death his children sold it. Between the years 1764—1805 it was an inn known as the Shoulder of Mutton. In the early 19th Century it became part of Park Hall estate owned by Captain Jack White. He bought the inn and returned it back to a parsonage. Later Jack White quarrelled with the parson and turned him out, and the building became an inn again, and has remained so ever since.

HEAGE

WHITE HART INN, HEAGE — 18th century coaching inn.

HIGHAM

CROWN INN, HIGHAM — Dates from the 15th century and a former coaching inn. Dick Turpin was reputed to have used the inn. See also the Bull Inn, Higham, in the Lost Inns section.

HILTON

OLD TALBOT INN, MAIN STREET, HILTON — 15th century inn with a controversial ghost.

HOLBROOK

SPOTTED COW, HOLBROOK — former farm building dating back to the 18th century.

HOLYMOORSIDE

LAMB INN, HOLYMOORSIDE — The building dates from 1760, but was not licensed until about 1850 when James Shemwell was the licensee. In 1953 the building was largely rebuilt. A tale was told years ago about a prank by one of the landlords. He invited everyone to come and see his water otter. Everyone assembled, expecting to see the animal, and being accompanied by their dogs. However the landlord showed them a kettle = the 'water hotter'!

HOPE

OLD HALL HOTEL, HOPE — As the name suggests, the building was originally Hope Hall of the Balguy family. In the 17th Century the Balguys owned several estates in the area, such as Derwent Hall, which was demolished in the 1940s and now lies beneath Ladybower

Reservoir. In St. Peter's Church, opposite the inn, in the chancel, is a small brass to Henry Balguy of Hope Hall. He died in 1685 and wears knee-breeches, doublet, conical hat, and holds a pen in one hand and a book in the other.

HULLAND WARD

BLACK HORSE INN, HULLAND WARD, NR. DERBY — 17th Century Inn on the main London to Manchester coach route. The inn also served as a tollgate.

I

ILKESTON

GALLOWS INN, ILKESTON — beside the Erewash Canal on the Derbyshire/Nottinghamshire boundary. As the name suggests, public hangings were carried out here.

GENERAL HAVELOCK, STANTON ROAD, ILKESTON — Named after General Havelock who with Sir James Outram retook the Residency in Lucknow with a small detachment in 1857, during the famous Indian Mutiny in 1857-8.

SHIPLEY BOAT INN, EREWASH CANAL, Nr. ILKESTON — Historically a very interesting area with the Shipley Lock on the Erewash Canal. Here boats were loaded with coal from the Shipley Collieries. In 1895 1,500 tons of coal a month was being loaded. The coal was brought in wagons down a railroad from the mines. The licencee of the Boat Inn supplied six horses to enable the wagons to be pulled back up the hill. A gallon of ale was allowed for each pair of loaded boats; a gang of six worked the wharf, averaging six boats per nine hour shift. Opposite the inn on the other side of the canal is The Slaughterhouse, which operated until 1962.

The inn was built in 1887. The Erewash Canal was built to serve the nearby coal mines, and runs for 11 miles from Langley Mill to the Trent at Sawley. It became operative from July 1779, and just in front of the inn are two locks.

INGELBY

JOHN THOMPSON, INGLEBY — a former farmhouse. Named after a go-ahead landlord who got fed up with farming and started a successful brewery instead.

K

KEDLESTON

KEDLESTON HOTEL, KEDLESTON — A Robert Adam building, which was for a while a derelict farmhouse. The building has been converted to a hotel and is owned by Lord

Scarsdale of Kedleston Hall. He in fact performed the opening ceremony in January 1971 and drove from the Hall in a coach and four. The Scarsdale family are the longest running continuous family to own an estate in Derbyshire, and the second longest in Britain.

KIRK IRETON

BULL'S HEAD, MAIN STREET, KIRK IRETON — Dates from 1709 and built using timbers from salvaged ships.

KIRK LANGLEY

MEYNELL ARMS HOTEL, ASHBOURNE ROAD, KIRK LANGLEY — Named after the Meynell estate, of which it was once part. The building is 300 years old and was a Mansion House. Known as Copestake House and now a Grade 11 listed building. The Meynell Hunt meet here.

KING'S NEWTON

THE HARDINGE ARMS, MAIN STREET, KING'S NEWTON. The building is 450 years old. Approximately 100 years an apple tree seedling was found growing in the guttering. From this has sprung the poular apple tree known as the Newton Wonder.

KNIVETON

THE GREYHOUND INN, KNIVETON — Like the Plough Inn in Ashbourne there are several footballs from the annual Ashbourne Shrovetide football match on display. The scorer of the goal is allowed to keep the ball as a souvenir of his effort. Among the balls here is one from the 1945 game.

KNOCKERDOWN

KNOCKERDOWN INN, KNOCKERDOWN, NR. ASHBOURNE — Formerly known as the Greyhound Inn. The inn sign illustrates a Roman figure and it is said that a former owner eventually knocked down the price and bought it!

L

LANGLEY MILL

GREAT NORTHERN, CANAL BASIN, LANGLEY MILL — Takes its name from the Great Northern Railway Company which once owned the now lost Nottingham Canal. The basin was where three canals met — The Cromford Canal to Cromford nr. Matlock Bath and Arwright's cotton spinning mill; the Nottingham Canal to the River Trent in central Nottingham; and the Erewash Canal from here to River Trent at Trent Lock. There are portions of the Nottingham Canal left and a four mile section of the Cromford Canal at

GALLOWS INN, ILKESTON  **FOX HOUSE INN, LONGSHAW**

GREAT NORTHERN, LANGLEY MILL

Cromford. The Erewash Canal has been restored and is navigable again. There are delightful canal side walks here and considerable local history to explore.

LEA

THE JUG AND GLASS INN, LEA, NR. MATLOCK — Lea and Holloway are renowned for their associations with the Nightingale family who resided at Lea Hurst, the most famous member of the family being Florence Nightingale, The Lady with the Lamp. It was Florence's uncle who in 1782 built an infirmary for employees of the Nightingale family. It was not until much later that the building became an inn.

LITTLE HAYFIELD

LANTERN PIKE, LITTLE HAYFIELD — A former farmhouse and originally known as the New Inn. Name later changed after the nearby hill where beacons were lit. An earlier landlady was murdered here in 1927 and the case was solved by the legendary Fabian of the Yard.

LITTLE HUCKLOW

OLD BULLS HEAD INN, LITTLE HUCKLOW — The inn dates from the 17th Century and is situated in an unusual village with no shop or church. The surrounding countryside bears evidence to the once prolific lead-mining industry. In the car park, on the inn walls, and inside the inn are a wealth of items of historical interest. Also inside is a cave, and it is claimed that Dick Turpin visited the inn.

LITTLE LONGSTONE

PACKHORSE INN, LITTLE LONGSTONE — The inn recently celebrated its 200th anniversary for on August 4th 1787 the owner described himself as a Miner and Inn Keeper. Lead mining was a major local industry in the area and packhorse teams frequently passed this way.

LONGSHAW

FOX HOUSE INN, LONGSHAW. G.R. 267804. — Situated just on the Derbyshire/South Yorkshire boundary. Dating back to the 17th Century, the inn was very popular with coaching traffic until 1895. That year the Totley Tunnel was opened, and the railway took most of the traffic. Today it is still a very popular inn, with the clientele coming largely from Sheffield. The origin of the name bears no resemblance to the animal. In the book, Place names of Derbyshire by K. Cameron, it is said to originate from Nicholas Fox in 1399. However, originally the building was built by Mr. Fox of Callow Farm, near Highlow Hall, south west of Hathersage. The Dukes of Rutland who owned the Longshaw estate until the 1930s extensively enlarged the building in the 1840s. For a while the inn was called The Traveller's Rest. A large room in the inn was often called the Duke's Room, since the Duke of Rutland occasionally slept there. In 1896 a group of shepherds met in the inn and decided to organise the first sheepdog trial, held in 1898. They have been held annually ever since at the beginning of September in the fields in front of Longshaw Lodge. The road junction outside the inn is believed to be the Whitcross (in Charlotte Bronte's book Jane Eyre) where Jane Eyre was set down from the coach during her flight north.

LULLINGTON

COLVILLE ARMS, LULLINGTON — 300 years ago this was a small inn with a cottage attached. Since then it has been combined and formed part of the Colville Estate. The exterior is 19th Century.

M

MAKENEY

HOLLY BUSH INN, MAKENEY — Former 17th century farmhouse with milestone outside; on the Derby Turnpike route. Grade 11 listed building.

MACKWORTH

MACKWORTH HOTEL, MACKWORTH — Built in 1860, this building was originally the village Post Office but has since been converted to an inn.

MARLPOOL

THE MUNDY ARMS, MARLPOOL Nr. HEANOR — The Mundy family are a prominent Derbyshire family whose origins go back to Saxon times. The name Mundy is Saxon meaning Moon Day or Monday. Through the centuries members of the family have played important roles locally and nationally. Sir John Mundy was Lord Mayor of London in 1522; Gilbert Mundy was Sheriff of Derbyshire in 1697; Edward Miller Mundy was an M.P. and High Sheriff of Derbyshire in 1772; and in the 19th Century members of the family rose to high military rank with Admiral Sir George Mundy and General Godfrey Basil Mundy. Other members of the family were born in the now destroyed Shipley Hall. Markeaton Hall, near Derby, was built by the Mundy family in 1755. There is a further Mundy Arms at Mackworth.

MATLOCK BATH

THE FISHPOND HOTEL, MATLOCK BATH — Situated opposite the Grand Pavilion, it takes its name from the fish pond opposite. The fish pond is fed by the thermal waters which once made Matlock Bath famous as a spa town. Living in the water are several fish, which seem to thrive on the thermal waters. Under the water of the fish pond is a milestone. It reads, Chatsworth 10 miles, Bakewell 10 miles, Manchester 45 miles, and is dated 1801.

THE NEW BATH HOTEL, MATLOCK BATH — Matlock Bath is renowned for its spa era. The first bath was built and paved in 1698. Another spring was discovered, and this hotel perpetuates its memory.

In a tourist guide dated 1802, the accommodation terms were — 5 shillings (25p) per week for a bed chamber, 14 shillings (70p) to one guinea (1.05p) for a private parlour, 1 shilling and 3 pence (6 p.) for breakfast, 2 shillings (10p) for dinner at the public table, 1 shilling (5p) for tea, and 1 shilling and 6 pence (7 p) for supper. Bathing was 6 pence (2 p) a time. Another tourist guide dated 1811 commented, The general cleanliness of the inns, lodging-houses and inhabitants, cannot escape the notice of travellers. In White's Derbyshire Directory of 1857, the following two verses about a lime tree in the grounds are detailed. The lime tree was said to be at least 150 years old, and the two verses were left on a table.

"Would you ask me the charms of the New Bath Inn;
There's a Linden tree grows in the garden so well,
That its branches o'er shadow a full rood of ground,
As you may prove clearly, if you'll only go round;
And its limbs are supported by forty-nine stakes,
Like the Banyan that grows by Hindoostan's lakes.

And the fountain moreover — aye, honour the Fountain,
That clear as the crystal bursts forth from the mountain;
All sparkling, and gushing, and limpid it flows,
And the Bath receives it as onward it goes.
'Tis a chosen retreat sure, the New Bath Inn,
There's beauty without, and there's comfort within."

In 1895 the hotel was described as furnished in a luxurious style. With the coming of the car age, in 1908, the hotel had a garage for four cars and an inspection pit. In 1871, the Emperor Dom Pedro II, Emperor of Brazil, and his wife, the Empress, stayed at the hotel on 10th August.

THE TEMPLE HOTEL, MATLOCK BATH — 18th Century sandstone building and a former coaching inn. Visited by several famous people, including Lord Byron who wrote a poem on a window pane. Princess Victoria (later Queen Victoria) came in 1832 and added her signature underneath the poem. It is reputed that the lounge inspired Rodgers to compose, There's a small hotel for Hammerstein.

MELBOURNE

ALMA INN, MELBOURNE — The building is about 500 years old. At one time it used to brew its own beer — for about 50 years — but does not do so any longer. The inn's name — Alma — which has only been used since the beginning of this century, is believed to derive from the battle of the River Alma in the Crimean War, on September 20th 1854.

SIR FRANCIS BURDETT, DERBY ROAD, MELBOURNE — The Burdett family built the nearby Foremark Hall, now part of Repton School. Sir Francis lived at the Hall and became an M.P. He later lost his seat by one vote. He built the splendid Jacobean church nearby dedicated to St. Saviour.

MILFORD BRIDGE

STRUTT ARMS, MILFORD — Opposite is the now closed cotton spinning mill founded by Jedediah Strutt in 1780.

STRUTT ARMS, MILFORD BRIDGE    THE HOBBIT INN, MONYASH

CROWN INN, HIGHAM

KING WILLIAM 1V INN, MILFORD — The third son of George 111 and born in 1765. In 1801 he was made Admiral of the Fleet. In June 1830 he succeeded his brother, George 1V., as King of Great Britain. He died in 1837.

MONYASH

THE HOBBIT INN — MONYASH — Dates from the 17th Century overlooking the Green and market cross. Formerly known as the Bull's Head.

N

NEWHAVEN

NEWHAVEN HOTEL, NEWHAVEN. ON A515 MIDWAY BETWEEN BUXTON AND ASHBOURNE — Prior to 1795 there was only one inn on the turnpike road from Buxton to Ashbourne. In 1705 this inn was built by the Duke of Devonshire, and was named the Devonshire Arms. It was known as a large handsome and commodious inn, where travellers meet with every requisite accommodation. There was originally sufficient stabling for 100 horses, and it was possibly the best-known hostelry in Derbyshire. One visitor to the inn was King George IV. He was said to have found everything to his liking, and as a result granted the inn a free and perpetual licence. In the 19th Century the inn became part of the Duke of Rutland's estate, and possibly the name of the inn was changed then.

NEW MILLS

BEE HIVE INN, NEW MILLS — a former toll house.

HARE AND HOUNDS INN, LOW LEIGHTON ROAD, NEW MILLS — Known locally as Newton's Folly, for originally it was built as a hunting lodge but the builder went bankrupt. In the cellar are two cells, remnants of the days when the building acted as a magistrates court.

PACKHORSE INN, MELLOR ROAD, NEW MILLS — as the inn sign records this was a popular resting place for packhorse teams before and after crossing the moorland areas. The inn is a converted farmhouse dated 1600.

NORTH WINGFIELD

BLUE BELL INN, North Wingfield. — Often referred to as the inn in the churchyard. The building is 15th century and was originally a Chantry House, established by Sir John Babington in 1488. St. Lawrence's church dates from Norman times and has a bell more than 300 years old. The Babington's are a well known Derbyshire family and renowned for the famous 'Babington' plot in the 16th Century, involving Mary, Queen of Scots, and Wingfield Manor at South Wingfield.

KING WILLIAM 1V, MILFORD BRIDGE    BARTLEWOOD LODGE, OCKBROOK

BLUE BELL INN, NORTH WINGFIELD

O

OAKERTHORPE

THE PEACOCK HOTEL, OAKERTHORPE, Nr South Wingfield. One of the oldest inns in Derbyshire with origins dating back to the 11th Century when it was known as Ufton Barn and mentioned in the Domesday Book. The tithe barn dates back to the 12th Century and was run by White Monks who offered food and lodging to travellers. The inn became an important halt in coaching days being on the main Sheffield-Derby road. The cost for servicing a coach and four was one shilling and six pence (7 p). The buildings still have many huge oak beams and four foot thick walls. Legends still are told of the tragic Mary, Queen of Scots, who was imprisoned nearby at Wingfield Manor. One recalls that she stayed here after escaping from the Manor along passageways cut by the White Monks for coal. But, there is no true evidence that she did! The road junction is a busy one and there were five inns here in the 19th century. The Crown Inn and the Gate Inn have gone, leaving the Peacock, Butchers Arms and The Anchor.

OCKBROOK

BARTLEWOOD LODGE, DALE ROAD, OCKBROOK — a converted 250 year old farmhouse. The moulded ceilings come from an earlier building.

P

PEAK FOREST

THE DEVONSHIRE ARMS HOTEL, PEAK FOREST. G.R. 115793. The Devonshire connection to the village lies opposite the inn, in the Church, dedicated to Charles, King and Martyr. This church was built in 1880, replacing a chapel built here in 1657 by Christina, the Countess of Devonshire. Her son, Charles Cavendish, was killed in July 1643, fighting for Charles the First, and is the reason why the Church is dedicated. The chapel in the first half of the 18th Century became very famous as the Gretna Green of the Midlands. At that time Peak Forest did not come under the jurisdiction of any Bishop. Consequently the vicar of Peak Forest had the following title — Principal Official and Judge in Spiritualities, in the Peculiar Court of Peak Forest. Between 1728-1754 about 100 runaway marriages were conducted here each year. In 1754 Lord Hardwick's Act put a stop to these marriages.

POMEROY

DUKE OF YORK, POMEROY, NR FLAGG — The building is 500 years old — a converted farmhouse — and formerly a coaching inn, situated on the busy A515 road, six miles from Buxton. The stables have now been incorporated as part of the bar complex.

Q

QUARNDON

THE JOINERS ARMS, QUARNDON — In 1869 the inn was granted a full licence. Three years previously, on October 23rd 1866, gas was laid to the village, and the first light to be lit was in the Joiners Arms. Two other inns existed in the 19th Century — the Pig and Whistle and the King's Head. Just down the road from the inn is the Chalybeate Spring. The water was known for its curative powers, but following an earth tremor in 1897 the water has never flowed since.

R

RENISHAW

SITWELL ARMS, STATION ROAD, RENISHAW — The Sitwells have long been associated with Renishaw. Their Hall — Renishaw Hall — dates from 1625. Many monuments to them can be seen in Eckington Church nearby.

Dr. Edith Sitwell (1887-1964) was a poet and writer. The most famous member of the family was Sir Osbert Sitwell (1892-1969), author of Left Hand, Right Hand. The Hall does have what is claimed to be the most northerly vineyard in the world, planted by Mr. Reresby Sitwell. In 1976 900 bottles of wine were produced.

REPTON

BOOT INN, 12 Boot Hill, REPTON — In approximately 1769 the building — house, garden and outbuildings — which occupied the site was demolished. A malthouse was built almost immediately upon the site and is today's building. Between 1840 — 1880 whilst still an inn, rooms were used for Petty Sessions, the Odd Fellows and Masonic Lodge. For much of the 19th Century it was privately owned, but in 1888 it was sold to Thomas Salt & Co (Brewers) of Burton on Trent. They in 1927 sold the inn to Bass Ratcliffe who later became Bass Holdings, who own it today. The landlord between 1938–1943 was a Mr. Pearson who committed suicide by gassin himself in the kitchen. The current landlord informed me — I am not about to do the same.!

THE BULL'S HEAD, REPTON — Formerly a coaching inn. The stables have now been demolished to allow more car parking space. The building has had several uses over the years, and for a while was a Post Office, while another part of the building was a bakehouse.

JOINERS ARMS, QUARNDON

THE BOOT INN, REPTON

BULLS HEAD, REPTON

PEACOCK HOTEL, ROWSLEY

RIDDINGS

MOULDER'S ARMS, CHURCH STREET, RIDDINGS — Known locally as the Thack it is the only thatched inn in Derbyshire.

THE SEVEN STARS, CHURCH STREET, RIDDINGS — dates from the 15th century.

ROWARTH

LITTLE MILL INN, ROWARTH — Built in 1781 and said to be haunted. The mill, which stood next to the inn, was destroyed in 1930 by a flood. The landlord of the inn was killed at the same time, as he had gone outside to look for his dog. In the grounds of the inn, until 1977, was a beautifully restored carriage from the 'Brighton Belle'. This served as a restaurant but was sold in 1977.

ROWSLEY

PEACOCK HOTEL, ROWSLEY — The datestone above the entrance is dated 1652 and refers to the time when the building was erected as a private residence for John Stevenson. He was man of affairs to Grace, Lady Manners, the mother of the 8th Earl of Rutland who founded the Bakewell School in 1636. The Rutland home is nearby — Haddon Hall. The peacock stands on the top of the Dukes of Rutland coat of arms. Up to 1828 there were two posting houses in Rowsley Square — The Nag's Head and the Red Lion. These were closed down, and the Peacock became a hotel. Inside the entrance can be seen a rare china peacock unearthed from a sunken ship.

S

SAWLEY

THE STEAMBOAT INN, TRENT LOCK, SAWLEY — Located beside the Erewash Canal and junction with the River Trent, the area was extremely busy with canal traffic at the end of the 19th century. The Bargees stayed here and their horses were stabled at the back in what is now the restaurant. The Wardroom, which can seat upto 120 people was the hay store! Upto World War 2 the inn was named, The Erewash Navigation Inn. From then until 1974 it was named, The Fisherman's Rest, and since then The Steamboat Inn. A ghost is said to haunt the restaurant and kitchen area, known as Ma Rice, after the Rice family who owned the inn for much of this century. When seen she asks for a pint of beer and only wants to pay 1t old pence for it! The inn has its own narrowboat and during the summer beer supplies are collected weekly by it. Often it is used for wedding parties who travel the last mile along the canal to inn, on the beautifully decked out boat. For canal lovers, like me, the inn is perfectly situated and a more pleasurable evening watching the traffic would be harder to find.

STEAMBOAT INN, TRENT LOCK, SAWLEY

MALT SHOVEL INN, SHARDLOW

NAVIGATION INN, TRENT LOCK (SAWLEY) — Beside the Erewash Canal at its junction with the River Trent. The grounds were used for prize-fighting and renowned fighters such as William Bendigo and Harry Poulson trained here.

SHARDLOW

THE MALT SHOVEL INN, SHARDLOW — Built in 1799 and, as the inn sign suggests, the building was originally the house of the manager of the Malthouse. The Malthouse now forms part of the licensed premises. Opposite this inn is another, named New Inn. The inn sign displays how the inn would have looked 200 years ago with the adjacent canal and barge being pulled by a horse.

These two inns form part of a very interesting 18th Century inland port, on the Trent and Mersey Canal built in 1777. Near the inn is a cast iron milepost on the towpath — Preston Brook 92 miles.

NEW INN, THE WHARF, SHARDLOW — Situated beside the Trent and Mersey Canal, the inn was originally a cottage built in 1779. Over the years the inn has been enlarged and now encompasses four cottages.

SHELDON

THE DEVONSHIRE ARMS, SHELDON, NR. BAKEWELL — (This Inn has now closed down.) A column in the Sheffield paper, The Star, on December 30th 1966, recalls the history of this inn. For at least 150 years, the Gyte family have run this inn. They farmed 182 acres at the back of the inn, and have been tenants of the inn since the end of the 18th Century. In 1866 they began purchasing their beer from Ind. Coope Limited, and were still doing so a hundred years ago. To mark the occasion Mrs. Alice Gyte, who ran the pub then, was presented with a silver tray. She could remember the days when people used to come in carts and on horses and tie them up on the iron rings outside, In 1966 they had no beer pumps and fetched the ale from the barrels in pint and quart jugs.

SHIRLEY

THE SARACEN'S HEAD INN, SHIRLEY — The village name would at first glance seem to have feminine origins, but in fact is derived from Schirleg, a 15th Century word meaning a clearing. The inn dates from 1791, and did in the 1970s have a female landlady whose surname was Shirley. The inn is named after the Crusades.

SHOTTLE

THE RAILWAY INN, COWERS LANE, SHOTTLE — At the junction of the B5023 and A517 road, the inn was originally a hunting lodge. In the 19th Century it was converted to an inn and named after the railway nearby, now disused, which extended to Wirksworth.

SMALLDALE

BOWLING GREEN INN, SMALLDALE, BRADWELL. G.R. 174818. — The inn dates back to the early 16th Century, and still retains its natural character. In the 18th Century the inn was sold twice for the princely sum of five shillings (25p) — the last time was in 1748, making it the cheapest inn in the county.

SNELSTON COMMON

QUEEN ADELAIDE, SNELSTON COMMON — a former farmhouse and named after William 1V's Queen who resided at Sudbury for several years.

SOUTH WINGFIELD

THE MANOR HOTEL, SOUTH WINGFIELD — A former coaching inn, known as the Horse and Groom.

YE OLDE YEW TREE INN, SOUTH WINGFIELD — An old timbered inn on the old Oakerthorpe to Ashbourne turnpike. The turnpike dates from the mid-18th Century and was 17 miles long.

SPARROWPIT

THE WANTED INN, SPARROWPIT, G.R. 091807. — The inn lies on the line of an old saltway which ran from Macclesfield through Chapel-en-le-Frith to Castleton and on to Sheffield via Stanedge Pole. The Inn is more than 400 years old, and was known for centuries as the Devonshire Arms. In 1956 it was put up for auction but was not sold. For two years the inn remained on the market but no-one wanted it. Finally it was purchased, and on October 27th, 1957, the then Minister of Works, The Rt. Hon. Hugh Molson, M.P., renamed it — The Wanted Inn, at the renaming ceremony.

SPONDON

THE MALT SHOVEL, POTTER STREET, SPONDON — The name records a local event which happened almost 650 years ago. In 1340 fire destroyed the malt house bringing about the Spondon Conflagration. Edward 111 exempted the village from paying any taxes until it was rebuilt.

STANLEY

WHITE HART, DERBY ROAD, STANLEY — dates from the 16th century.

STANTON IN PEAK

FLYING CHILDERS INN, STANTON IN PEAK — The building dates from the 17th Century, and was formerly four cottages. In the early 1700s they were converted to an inn. The unusual inn name is from a famous racehorse owned by the Duke of Devonshire. It was reputed to be the fleetest in the world and died in 1741, aged 26 years.

STRETTON

HIDE-A-WAY INN, STRETTON — Built about 160 years ago, the inn was originally named The North Midland Railway Hotel, being near a railway line and station. At one time there was a smithy and house attached to the inn.

STONEY MIDDLETON

THE MOON INN, STONEY MIDDLETON — In 1750 a Scottish pedlar is said to have been murdered in the inn. He had been to Eyam Fair and noticed several others selling goods without a licence. He informed the Police, who removed the protesting pedlars. They later got their revenge. His body was taken on horseback and dumped well inside Carlswark Cavern nearby. It was about twenty years later that his skeleton was found. For a long while it was kept in a box in Eyam Church, before being buried in the churchyard. His body had been identified by the intricate buckles on his shoes. The five 'murderers' were never caught, but the last one told the story just before dying peacefully.

THE ROYAL OAK, THE DALE, STONEY MIDDLETON — dates from the 16th Century and in the 18th Century frequented by murderers. See also the Moon Inn in Stoney Middleton.

SUDBURY

THE VERNON ARMS, SUDBURY — The Vernons, a branch of the Vernon family from Haddon Hall near Bakewell, have long been associated with Sudbury. The Hall (now National Trust property) was built by Sir George Vernon from 1660 onwards. On a map dated 1659 an inn is shown, but the present building was not built until 1671. It proved to be a popular coaching inn, and was a coaching stage. The stables still remain. In the 18th and 19th Centuries the Red Rover on the Manchester to London run generally reached the inn at 10 a.m. The north-bound coach arrived at about 4 p.m. With the coming of the railway in the 1850s the coaching scene soon disappeared. The Vernons often used the inn for public dinners. A walk round Sudbury village is well worthwhile to see the stocks and late 19th Century butcher's shop.

SWADLINCOTE

CATCHEMS INN, SWADLINCOTE — The name is said to derive from a former landlord, named Ketcham. A tale is told that, as the toll gate was very close to the inn, the people paying the toll generally stopped at the inn en route. As a result Mr. Ketcham used to catch 'em!

SWARKSTONE

CREWE AND HARPUR ARMS, SWARKSTONE — An inn has stood on this site for the last 800 years. The present building was built in 1744. Standing at the junction of A574 and A5009 roads, and close to the famous Swarkstone Bridge, the inn was a popular resting place. The stables from the coaching days have now been converted to garages.

THE WANTED INN, SPARROWPIT

HIDE-A-WAY INN, STRETTON

VERNON ARMS, SUDBURY

GEORGE HOTEL, TIDESWELL

T

TAXAL

THE CHIMES OF TAXAL, TAXAL. G.R. 006798. Situated at the northern end of the Goyt Valley, the inn dates back to the 17th Century. Until 1936 Taxal was part of Cheshire, but that year the boundaries were readjusted and it is now in Derbyshire. Originally the inn was named The Royal Oak, but recently has been changed to the Chimes of Taxal. Originally built as a hunting lodge for Charles 11; not an inn until 1829. The name Taxal does not refer to a place where taxes were paid; instead the name comes from Tata who married Edwin, King of Northumbria, in the 7th Century.

THORPE

DOG AND PARTRIDGE HOTEL, THORPE — An old coaching inn some 250 years old.

TICKNALL

STAFF OF LIFE, TICKNALL — Formerly named the Loaf of Bread as bread was made here and is now depicted on the sign. Part of the lounge was the bakery. Also in the village the Chequers Inn dates from the 17th century with beamed ceilings and is the oldest public house in Ticknall. The Wheel Inn was in existance in 1846 when three inns and four beer houses served a population of 1,271. Today's population is about 540.

TIDESWELL

ANCHOR INN, NR. TIDESWELL. G.R. 160764. — The building is about 500 years old and has witnessed the growth of transport through the ages. At first it was a Farm House, later a Packhorse Halt and finally a coaching inn.

FIRST DROP INN, OLD MARKET PLACE, TIDESWELL — The inn's name is one of the most apt and unusual in Derbyshire. The Dining Room is named The Drunken Butcher after a ballad by William Bennett. He lived in Tideswell in the late 18th century and apart from owning a weaving factory he was a popular poet. Two of his well known ballads are The Cavalier and The King of the Peak. The Drunken Butcher ballad is the story of a butcher who, following a drunken party at Sparrowpit, was chased over the moors by a ghost, as he rode home to Tideswell.

THE GEORGE HOTEL, TIDESWELL — Situated beside the magnificent 14th Century Cathedral of the Peak, the inn dates back to 1730 and is an attractive building with venetian windows and oak-panelled lounges. In the 18th Century the inn was held in high esteem by 18th Century travellers, for the coaching inn was a regular stopping point on the turnpike from Sheffield to Buxton. Originally there were extensive stables, but these have now been converted to other uses.

In 1810 Bernard Bird, a Sheffield journalist, came to Tideswell to gather material for a book on the Peak District. He wrote -

> "When I first came to Tideswell in the year 1810, I lodged at the hotel kept by Nanny Royston. I had a comfortable bed and frequently the company from all nations (including fiddlers, pipers, and travelling organists) and the house resounded with merriment every night. I have heard that the inhabitants on the Lancashire side bear an indifferent character, but in my dealings with the people of Tideswell generally, I have found them respectable and upright in all matters, equal if not superior to any people in the Kingdom."

Inside the inn is a picture of the local Catch and Gee Club members singing around a piano. Two of the members — Samuel Slack and William Newton (the Minstrel of the Peak) are buried in Tideswell churchyard. William Newton was born in Tideswell in 1750.

TURNDITCH

THE CROSS KEYS INN, TURNDITCH — Formerly the building was private houses, but in more recent times has been converted to an inn, providing a distinct olde worlde atmosphere.

TUNSTEAD MILTON

ROSE AND CROWN INN, TUNSTEAD MILTON, NR. WHALEY BRIDGE — 17th Century building. Near the inn are remains of a millstone which, for a long while, was known as Tunstead Millstone — hence today's village name.

TWO DALES

THE PLOUGH INN — TWO DALES — Dates from the 18th century — the date stone is above the door — 1751 — and a former coaching inn. Sydnope Hill was a notorious route from Chesterfield over the moors, as it is today, being steep, narrow and twisty. Two Dales was a welcome refreshment stop before or after the hill. There were several inns here but the Plough is the only one remaining. The Nag's Head was close by in the courtyard and beside the road was the Blacksmith's Arms near the old Smithy.

W

WARDLOW

BULLS HEAD INN, WARDLOW, NR. TIDESWELL — An old coaching inn dating back to the beginning of the 17th Century. Several trading routes passed this way, including

MANOR HOTEL, SOUTH WINGFIELD

YEW TREE INN, SOUTH WINGFIELD

THREE STAGS HEADS, WARDLOW MIRES

THREE HORSE SHOES INN, WESSINGTON

packhorse ways and The Portway. One route went from Ashford via Eyam to Hathersage. Another ran from Wardlow to Hassop, Pilsley and Bakewell. Where these two crossed east of Wardlow is a lane known as Black Harry Lane. Highwaymen were a constant threat to packhorse teams. One was active in this area and was known as Black Harry. He was finally caught, and later hung and gibbeted at Wardlow Mires (G.R. 181756). An account of this can be seen at the inn. Wardlow Mires was a popular gibbeting area. One of the last gibbets in England occurred here on April 1st, 1815. Anthony Lingard had murdered the tollkeeper (there was a toll house at Wardlow Mires) and was later caught and sentenced in Derby.

WESSINGTON

THE HORSE AND JOCKEY, THE GREEN, WESSINGTON — Former coaching inn, built in 1683.

THREE HORSE SHOES INN, WESSINGTON — As the inn's name suggests, the building was once a blacksmith's forge and stables, and dates from the beginning of the 17th Century. Horse trading was carried out here until this century, and ponies were often sold in the tap room.

WEST HALLAM

THE WHITE HART, WEST HALLAM — Dates from the 17th Century, and was originally a farmhouse licensed to sell ale. It was also a host house to the Benedictine monks of Dale Abbey, of which only a window and some masonry remains today.

WHALEY BRIDGE

JODRELL ARMS HOTEL, WHALEY BRIDGE — A former coaching inn, the inn takes its name from the Jodrell family, who from 1206 onwards owned much of the area. The inn was built in the 1690's and has a fine Tuscan porch. Grade 11 listed building.

WHATSTANDWELL

THE DERWENT HOTEL, WHATSTANDWELL — Named after the River Derwent, which flows on the lefthand side, its original name was Bulls Head. The beautifully ivy-clad inn is beside a bridge over the Derwent. During coaching days the inn was on an old turnpike, and the coaches used to stop here before setting off up the hill to Whatstandwell and Crich. Among the coaches calling here in 1846 were the Mail between Manchester and Derby, the Peak Guide betwen Ambergate and Buxton, and the Champion between Manchester and Nottingham.

The name of the village, Whatstandwell, which lies to the east of the inn, is from Walter Stonewell, who built a bridge here in the 14th Century. In the early 19th Century it was marked on the map as Hot-Stanwell and later that century it was known locally as Will't stand well?.

WILLINGTON

WILLINGTON HOUSE HOTEL, 28 HALL LANE, WILLINGTON — An unusual building, as the front does not face the road but the extensive gardens and River Trent.

WINDLEY

PUSS IN BOOTS, WINDLEY — The building dates from 1686, but how the inn received its name is not known. The double-sided inn sign portrays the famous pantomime of a cat carrying his belongings at the end of a stick over his shoulder. On his feet he elegantly wears a pair of turned-down wellingtons.

On the other side of the sign is the following poem:-

> The water kindly turns the mill
> While I grind corn for many
> And ale, I hope may further still
> Assist to turn the penny.
>
> Then try, my lads, how soon or late.
> How ale your strength recruits.
> You'll ever find a cheering bate
> With honest Puss in Boots.

WINGERWORTH

THE HUNLOKE ARMS, WINGERWORTH — During the Civil War the Hunlokes along with many other leading Derbyshire families supported the Royalist cause. As the inn sign records, a Hunloke was knighted at Edgehill in 1642. He was later made a Lieutenant of the County by James 11.

WINSTER

THE BOWLING GREEN, EAST BANK, WINSTER — One of only three inns in Winster. In 1750 there were more than twenty when lead mining was a big industry and the population of the village rose to over 2000. (See Lost Inns section for further details about Winster. Until early this century cattle fairs were held outside the inn on East Bank).

THE HALL, WINSTER — now an inn, but built by Francis Moore in 1628. A white lady is said to haunt the grounds! According to the legend, a daughter of the house fell in love with the coachman. The parents would not agree to the marriage, so one day they climbed to the top of the building and, swearing true love, they held hands and jumped to their deaths.

PUSS IN BOOTS, WINDLEY    MINERS STANDARD, WINSTER

MINERS STANDARD, WINSTER — The inn was built in 1653, and the name refers to the standard dish that was used to measure lead ore. Winster was formerly part of a very rich mining area. A standard dish made in 1512 is kept in the Moot Hall, Wirksworth. The dish holds about 13 Winchester pints. Nine dishes — one load; 12 loads — one fother (about 22 cwts.). (See also Pig of Lead inn, near Bonsall.)

As you enter the inn, over the main doorway can be seen the date 1653 and the initials E.P.; E.P.; F.P. They stand for Edith, Ella and Frank Price. Locally the initials are said to mean, Every person entering pays for a pint! The inn sign depicts lead mining equipment.

WIRKSWORTH

BLACK'S HEAD INN, MARKET PLACE, WIRKSWORTH — more than 250 years old.

HOPE AND ANCHOR INN, WIRKSWORTH — Former Govenor's residence when Wirksworth was a convict town. The lounge bar has a particularly fine Jacobean fireplace. The ceilings on the first floor contain Jacobean moulded panels.

THE KING'S FIELD INN — WIRKSWORTH — While being a new inn the sign and name recall Wirksworth's past for the town was a major lead mining centre from Roman times. The surrounding area was known as the King's Field covering an area of 73,800 acres. The name Kingàs Field originates from the Sovereign who, as the Duke of Lancaster, is entitled to a proportion of all mined lead.

RED LION INN — WIRKSWORTH — An impressive coaching and posting inn with parts dating back to the 16th Century, particularly the buttressed stone chimney on the Matlock road side. In 1750 it was partly rebuilt and the present front was added.

YOULGREAVE

THE BULL'S HEAD, YOULGREAVE — 16th Century building and a former coaching inn.

LOST INNS

Many of the small villages of Derbyshire, and especially the villages in the lead-mining districts of the Peak District, had numerous inns in the 18th Century. To illustrate this point we look at the villages of Winster and Crich. A small selection of 'lost inns' is detailed at the end.

WINSTER

In a census of tavern owners in Derbyshire in 1577, Winster was found to have "no taverns, inn or alehouse". In the 18th Century Winster became an important lead-mining centre, and the population of 600 rose to over 2,000. In 1750 there were more than twenty inns; today there are only two! The reduction was brought about by the decline in lead mining. In the 1760s six inns closed, leaving only eighteen.

Near the Post Office on the Main Street are the buildings which were formerly the Crown Inn but are now a private house. Opposite the Market House is the Angel Inn, also now a private house. This particular inn had a ghost, and stories are still told about her being a headless bride. Why she should be headless is not known. One story refers to a woman upstairs sitting in front of a mirror combing her hair. While she was doing this she suddenly noticed a headless bride walking up the stairs and into her room. She screamed before fainting.

On West Bank, below Bank House, is the former Shoulder of Mutton Inn. Postcards are still kept by the author showing West Bank and the inn with the hanging sign. The two inns which are left are the Bowling Green Inn on East Bank and the Miner's Standard at the south-western end of the village.

CRICH

Crich has a better record than Winster. In 1846 there were 11 inns and 13 beerhouses. At least ten have now ceased functioning and are private houses or have been pulled down. Crich had a more stable industry, with villagers being involved in wool and cotton spinning, lead mining, agriculture and quarrying. There was no boom as there was at Winster. One of the 'lost inns' was The Wheatsheaf at the top of Sheaf Lane. It is now a private house, and the old brewhouse can be seen opposite. A relative of George Stevenson used to own it. Another was the Bull's Head, likewise a private house after closing its doors in 1955. The building dates back to the 12th Century, and was first occupied by the masons building the parish church. The stables are now a garage. The White Swan was in the Market Place and was linked to the Black Swan (which is still operating) by an underground passage. The Miner's Hack was situated at Wakebridge and is now a private house. The lead miners used to receive their wages here. In the Royal Oak Cottages was an inn known as the Royal Oak. Nothing remains to be seen of the inn, although a few years ago the bar and wall bench seating were still in situ.

The inns still operating in the Crich area are the Jovial Dutchman, the Derwent Hotel (at Whatstandwell), the Black Swan, Canal Inn, Cliff Inn and the Rising Sun.

THE ASHOPTON INN
Ashopton.

One of the more recent 'lost inns'. When Ladybower Reservoir was being built — 1935 – 45 — the villages of Derwent and Ladybower were demolished. The inn was one of the buildings to be pulled down. The site of the inn is beside the Ashopton Viaduct.

THE BULL
Higham. G.R. 290590

The inn is now Bull Farm, but was formerly a popular coaching inn. Coaches travelling between Sheffield and Derby changed their horses here. Dick Turpin is reputed to have visited the inn.

THE COCK AND PYNOT INN
Whittington, Chesterfield. G.R. 384749

The Armorial Bearings of the Borough of Chesterfield include a cock and pynot. A pynot is the local name for magpie. They are included in the Bearings because a major event took place in 1688 in the Cock and Pynot Inn. Here in the Inn's parlour met the 4th Earl of Devonshire, the Earl of Danby and John D'Arcy, heir to the Earl of Holderness. The plan that hatched between them led to the Glorious Revolution in November 1688. King James II fled the country and William of Orange took over. In May 1694 the Earl of Devonshire was made a Duke for his part in the revolution. The inn was a long low thatched building with an inn sign, like the gallows sign in Ashbourne, hung across the road. By the beginning of this century there was little left of the inn, and what was left was being used as a house. To celebrate the 250th anniversary of the Revolution the house was brought back to its former state, and the tenth Duke of Devonshire, on October 28th 1938, officially opened the building as a museum. Her Grace the Dowager Duchess of Devonshire had a copy of the àplotting chairà made, and it was presented to the museum in 1938. The original, which the Earl of Devonshire is said to have sat upon, is in Hardwick Hall. The museum is open during the summer months only.

DALE in South Derbyshire, east of Derby.

Renowned for its ruined abbey and hermit's cave; the village once had The Flourish Inn and The Blue Bell Inn. The most famous of them all is the church dedicated to All Saints. The church dates from 1480, and is only 26 ft. by 25 ft. The other half of the building is a farm house. This farm house was at one time an inn.

THE DEAN OF HARTINGTON'S ARMS
Nr. Newhaven. G.R. 166588

Today this is Bank House Farm, but in the 19th Century it was a coaching inn. On the 1840 O.S. map it is shown as the 'Dean of Arlington's Arms'. It was in fact the Hartington's Arms, and the Deanery was abolished in 1858. The coat of arms above the porch dated 1856 is not the Dean's, but T.O. Bateman's of Middleton of Youlgreave, who purchased the inn.

THE OLD STAR
Loads, Nr. Holymoorside.

Up to the early part of the 19th Century the village of Loads was the principal habitation, with Holymoorside a relatively small hamlet. Today it is the reverse, with Loads being a scattering of houses. The Old Star is believed to have been licensed in 1821 and surrendered its licence in 1959.

PEAK CAVERN INN
Castleton.

Perhaps the oddest inn in Derbyshire. The cavern entrance is the largest in Britain, and for several centuries until the 1970s was used for ropemaking and has five ropewalks. It is recorded that in 1794 there was a public house inside the cavern. It was a place where the sun never shone and the rain never fell.

PIKEHAM INNE
Pikehall. G.R. 193591

This inn is marked on Ogilby's map of 1675 and is on the Derby to Manchester road. Today it is Pikehall Farm, with a barrel-arched cellar.

CANAL TAVERN
Shardlow.

A 19th Century building which now faces the lock house, formerly the Canal Tavern. The building stands on the site of a warehouse which served the River Trent behind the house and was built before the Trent and Mersey Canal. The present house once had its own bakery and slaughter-house. The inn was famous for the singing led by a famous narrow boatman named L.T.C. Rolt. The area was known as "Singing Shardlow". On Canal Bank Road, Shardlow, is Holden House. This was formerly a public house named Holden House.

FORMER FLOURISH INN, NR DALE

LIST OF INNS AND VISIT RECORD CHART —

DATE VISITIED

(A)

ALDERWASLEY   Ye Olde Bear Inn..

ALFRETON   Angel Hotel..

AMBERGATE   Excavator Inn...
                         Hurt Arms Hotel..

ASHBOURNE   Green Man Hotel...
                         The Plough Inn..
                         Smith's Tavern..
                         Wellington Inn..

ASHOPTON WOODLANDS   Snake Inn..

ASHOVER   Crispin Inn..
                         Greyhound Inn...

ASHFORD IN THE WATER Bull's Head..

(B)

BAKEWELL   Castle Hotel..
                         Manners Inn..
                         Queen's Arms Hotel..
                         Red Lion Inn..
                         Rutland Arms Hotel...

BAMFORD   Ladybower Inn..
                         Marquis of Granby Inn..

BARLBOROUGH   De Rodes Arms...

BASLOW   Cavendish Hotel..
                         Robin Hood Inn...

BEELEY   Devonshire Arms...

BELPER   Duke of Devonshire..
                         The King's Head...
                         Imperial Vaults..
                         Lion Hotel...
                         Lord Nelson...
                         Railway Tavern...
                         Rifleman's Arms..
                         Talbot Hotel..

BIRCH VALE   Waltzing Weasel...

BIRCHOVER   Druid Inn..
                         Red Lion Inn..

66

BOLSOVER	Castle Inn ....
	White Swan ....
BONSALL	Kings Head ....
	Pig of Lead ....
BORROWASH	Wilmot Arms ....
BRADWELL	Shoulder of Mutton ....
BRAILSFORD	Rose & Crown ....
BRASSINGTON	Ye Olde Gate Inn ....
BRETTON	Barrel Inn ....
BROUGH	Traveller's Rest ....
BUXTON	Bull i' th' Thorn ....
	Cat & Fiddle Inn ....
	Old Hall Hotel ....
	The Cheshire Cheese ....
	Ye Olde Sun Inn ....
	Old Swan Inn ....
	King's Head Hotel ....

Ⓒ

CASTLETON	Bull's Head ....
	Castle Hotel ....
	Ye Olde Nag's Head ....
CHAPEL EN LE FRITH	Dog Inn ....
	Jolly Carter ....
	Royal Oak ....
CHESTERFIELD	Ye olde Angel Hotel ....
	Blue Stoops Inn ....
	Ye Olde Crooked Spire ....
	Golden Fleece ....
	Market Hotel ....
	Peacock Inn (Centre) ....
	Portland Hotel ....
	Royal Oak ....
	Welbeck Inn ....
CHINLEY	Old Hall Hotel ....
CHINLEY HEAD	Lamb Inn ....
CLAY CROSS	George and Dragon ....
CLIFTON (Nr Ashbourne)	Cock Inn ....
COMBS	Old Bee Hive Inn ....
	Hanging Gate Inn ....

CRICH	Jovial Dutchman Inn..
CROMFORD	Boat Inn ....
	Greyhound Hotel ....
CROWDICOTE	Packhorse Inn..
CUBLEY	Howard Arms...

(D)

DARLEY ABBEY	The Abbey..
DARLEY BRIDGE	Square and Compass...
	Three Stags Head..
DARLEY DALE	Whitworth Hotel ....
DERBY	Bell Hotel...
	Broadway...
	Bell and Castle Inn ....
	Duke of Clarence...
	The Dolphin Inn ....
	Exeter Arms ....
	The Friary Hotel ....
	Mr. Jorrocks..
	Maypole Inn..
	Ye Olde Spa Inne...
	Old Silk Mill ....
	The Seven Stars Inn ....
	Wardwick Tavern..
DETHICK	White Hart Inn ....
DRONFIELD	Blue Stoops...
	Green Dragon ....
	Hyde Park Inn...
	White Swan ....
DUFFIELD	King's Head...
	Patternmakers Arms ....

(E)

EARL STERNDALE	Quiet Woman..
EDALE	The Old Nag's Head..
	The Rambler Inn...
EDNASTON	Yew Tree Inn..
ETWALL	The Spread Eagle..

EYAM	Bull's Head Hotel
	Miners' Arms

F

FLAGG	The Plough Inn
FOOLOW	The Lazy Landlord
FROGGATT EDGE	The Chequers Inn
FENNY BENTLEY	Coach & Horses Inn
FURNESS VALE	Soldier Dick

G

GLAPWELL	Young Vanish Inn
GLOSSOP	Grouse Inn
GRINDLEFORD	Maynard Arms Hotel
	Sir William Hotel
GREAT LONGSTONE	Crispin Inn

H

HADFIELD	Peels Arms
HARDSTOFT	The Shoulder of Mutton
HARTINGTON	Charles Cotton Hotel
HASSOP	Eyre Arms
HATHERSAGE	George Hotel
	Hathersage Inn
	Little John Hotel
	Millstone Inn
	Scotsman's Pack Inn
HAYFIELD	Royal Hotel
	George Hotel
	Pack Horse Inn
HEAGE	White Hart Inn
HIGHAM	Crown Inn
HILTON	Old Talbot
HOLBROOK	Spotted Cow
HOLYMOORSIDE	Lamb Inn

HOPE	Old Hall Hotel
HULLAND WARD	Black Horse Inn

I

ILKESTON	Gallows Inn
	General Havelock
	Shipley Boat Inn
INGELBY	John Thompson

K

KEDLESTON	Kedleston Hotel
KIRK IRETON	Bull's Head
KIRK LANGLEY	Meynell Arms Hotel
KING'S NEWTON	The Hardinge Arms
KNIVETON	Greyhound Inn
KNOCKERDOWN	Knockerdown Inn

L

LANGLEY MILL	Great Northern
LEA	Jug and Glass Inn
LITTLE HAYFIELD	Lantern Pike
LITTLE HUCKLOW	Old Bulls Head Inn
LITTLE LONGSTONE	Packhorse Inn
LONGSHAW	Fox House Inn
LULLINGTON	Colville Arms

M

MAKENEY	Holly Bush Inn
MACKWORTH	Mundy Arms
	Mackworth Hotel
MARLPOOL (Nr Heanor)	Mundy Arms
MATLOCK BATH	Fishpond Hotel
	New Bath Hotel
	Temple Hotel

MELBOURNE	Alma Inn... Sir Francis Burdett ....
MILFORD BRIDGE	King William IV... Strutt Arms...
MONYASH	The Hobbit Inn...

(N)

NEWHAVEN	Newhaven Hotel...
NEW MILLS	Bee Hive Inn.. Hare and Hounds Inn... Packhorse Inn..
NORTH WINGFIELD	Blue Bell Inn...

(O)

OAKERTHORPE	Peacock Inn .... Anchor Inn ....
OCKBROOK	Bartlewood Lodge ....

(P)

PEAK FOREST	Devonshire Arms ....
POMEROY (FLAGG)	Duke of York ....

(Q)

QUARNDON	The Joiners Arms...

(R)

RENISHAW	Sitwell Arms Hotel...
REPTON	Bull's Head .... Boot Inn ....
RIDDINGS	Moulder's Arms.. Seven Stars ....
ROWARTH	Little Mill Inn...
ROWSLEY	Peacock Hotel..

(S)

SAWLEY (Trent Lock)	Steamboat Inn .... Navigation Inn...

SHARDLOW	Malt Shovel Inn
	New Inn
SHELDON	Devonshire Arms
SHIRLEY	Saracen's Head Inn
SHOTTLE	The Railway Inn
SMALLDALE	Bowling Green Inn
SNELSTON COMMON	Queen Adelaide
SOUTH WINGFIELD	The Manor Hotel
	Ye Olde Yew Tree Inn
SPARROWPIT	The Wanted Inn
SPONDON	Malt Shovel Inn
STANLEY	White Hart
STANTON IN PEAK	Flying Childers Inn
STRETTON	Hide-A-Way Inn
STONEY MIDDLETON	Moon Inn
	Royal Oak
SUDBURY	Vernon Arms
SWADLINCOTE	Catchems Inn
SWARKSTONE	Crewe & Harpur Arms

T

TAXAL	Chimes of Taxal
THORPE	Dog & Partridge Hotel
TICKNALL	Staff of Life
TIDESWELL	Anchor Inn
	First Drop Inn
	George Hotel
TURNDITCH	Cross Keys Inn
TUNSTEAD MILTON	Rose & Crown Inn
TWO DALES	The Plough Inn

W

WARDLOW	Bulls Head Inn
WESSINGTON	Horse & Jockey
	Three Horse Shoes Inn

WEST HALLAM	The White Hart
WHALEY BRIDGE	Jodrell Arms Hotel
WHATSTANDWELL	Derwent Hotel
WILLINGTON	Willington House Hotel
WINDLEY	Puss in Boots
WINGERWORTH	The Hunloke Arms
WINSTER	Miners Standard
	The Bowling Green
	The Hall
WIRKSWORTH	Black's Head
	The King's Field
	Red Lion Inn
	Malt Shovel Inn
	Hope and Anchor Inn

Y

YOULGREAVE	The Bulls Head Inn

FORMER BULL'S INN, HIGHAM